ICE CREAM COOK[illegible]K

HOMEMADE ICE CREAM, GELATO, SHERBET, AND FROZEN YOGURT RECIPES WITH AND WITHOUT AN ICE CREAM MAKER

LOUISE DAVIDSON

ISBN: 9798672441504

Printed in the United States.

www.thecookbookpublisher.com

CONTENTS

MAKING ICE CREAM AT HOME!

We all know the quote "I scream. You scream. We all scream for one thing – Ice cream!" Isn't true that when the weather becomes nice, the first thing we do is to get some ice cream! The great thing is that you can easily make homemade ice cream in your kitchen and bring happiness all around you. It's much easier than you think and you can always make your favorite without any of added preservation agents or other chemicals we cannot pronounce. You will never go back to store-bought ice cream again!

In this cookbook, you will find frozen dairy desserts recipes for ice cream, gelato, sherbet, and frozen yogurt.

Ice Cream: as its name says, is a sweet frozen dessert (or snack) which is made with cream, milk, sugar (or other forms of sweetener) and some type of flavoring like vanilla, chocolate, fruits, coffee, etc. it can also include egg yolks and can be cooked before being transformed into ice cream.

Gelato is the Italian name for ice cream. Although ice cream and gelato look similar there are several differences between the two including:

- Ice cream has a higher fat content, it usually contains a higher ratio of cream to milk whereas gelato has more milk than cream content. This means more cream versus milk in ice cream. Ice cream needs at least 10% content of fat by law (USDA) whereas gelato only has 5-7% of fat content. Another difference in ingredients is concerning eggs. Ice cream recipes often call for egg yolks whereas gelato rarely has eggs.

- The churning process is also different. The churning is what makes the ice cream and gelato creamy. Ice cream is churned at a more rapid speed than gelato which means that gelato is creamier and has a denser texture than ice cream which contains more air, about 50% because of the rapid churning process. Gelato usually has about 25 to 30% of air.

- Another difference is that gelato is often served a higher temperature than ice cream, making it feel creamier and softer.

Sherbet is somewhat the distant parent of sorbet (pureed fruits, sweetener, and water) but with dairy ingredients added to its base. It usually contains 1 or 2% fat content, making it a creamy dessert similar to ice cream and gelato. It's a good choice for a healthier alternative to ice cream and gelato. The flavoring for sherbet is mostly fruit-based whereas ice cream and gelato have many flavors that are not only fruit-based like sherbets.

Frozen yogurt is made the same way as ice cream but instead of cream and milk in its base, it has yogurt, usually plain yogurt to which you add flavoring as you do with ice cream. Frozen yogurt has therefore a lower level of fat content and is often considered the healthier alternative.

Equipment

To do most recipes in this cookbook, you will need basic equipment like bowls, a handheld electric mixer, a spoon or whisk, and some recipes will ask for a blender for making the fruit puree to flavor up the base of your frozen dessert. If you are making your ice cream manually, you will also need a 9x13-inch glass (Pyrex) or stainless steel deep pan that you will place in the freezer. A bowl with a spout like a 2 or 3-quart glass measuring cup with a spout can be quite useful to pour the base into the ice cream maker or the pan. You can also invest in an electric ice cream maker, which will do all the churning processes for you and will save time and will result in good texture every time. Most ice cream makers on the market will have different speeds of churning and often have different options such as ice cream, gelato, and frozen yogurt, making it super easy to make ice cream at home.

The ice cream-gelato-sherbet bases are made with milk and/or heavy cream, sugar, and flavoring and if you are using the custard method, you will need some egg yolks to temper them with the hot, heavy cream mixture. The most important thing is to let the whole mixture cools completely before pouring it into the ice cream maker. Depending on the brand you are using, it will take 25-35 minutes to make smooth frozen homemade ice cream. After that, you can serve it softly frozen or place it in the freezer for a harder texture and serve it later. If you have an ice cream that has hardened, allow it to sit at room temperature for 10-15 minutes before serving and easily make nice scoops, especially if it is very hard.

If you don't have an ice cream maker, what I would recommend is using the ice cream base, flavor it with your favorite flavors, and pour it in a freezer-safe 9x13-inch baking pan made of glass-like Pyrex or stainless steel as it has to be a freezer-safe pan. You will need to freeze it up for at least 4 hours before serving, but what is important in this process is to churn it every 30 minutes, so it freezes up evenly. It's more effort to make homemade ice cream this way, but it will work fine and will result in the perfect scoop of homemade ice cream, gelato, sherbet, or frozen yogurt that you will be proud to serve to your family or friends.

Whether you choose to work with custard or not, the most important thing is to use a chilled ice cream base to go further with it. After your base is made, it very important to chill it in the refrigerator covered with plastic wrap for at least 2 hours. Overnight (8-12 hours) will give you the best results as the flavors will have time to develop even more.

ICE CREAM RECIPES

Easy Vanilla Ice Cream

Makes about 4 cups (½ cup per serving)

Ingredients
¾ cup granulated sugar
2 cup heavy whipping cream
1 cup milk
2 teaspoons vanilla extract

Directions
<u>*With an ice cream maker*</u>

1. Freeze the ice cream maker bowl according to manufacturer instructions, usually 12 to 24 hours.
2. Meanwhile in a large saucepan, add the whole milk, heavy cream, and sugar. Stir to combine.
3. Over medium-low heat, bring the mixture to a soft simmering and whisk constantly until the sugar is completely dissolved, about 10-12 minutes.
4. Pour the mixture in a clean bowl, preferably with a spout. Stir in the vanilla extract and let cool to room temperature.
5. Cover with plastic wrap and place in the refrigerator for at least 2 to 12 hours.
6. Pull out the ice cream mixture from the refrigerator and stir a few times.
7. Install the frozen ice cream maker bowl and pour the mixture into the ice cream maker. Connect the machine and press ice cream and the start button.
8. When the cycle is finished, transfer the ice cream to an airtight freezer-safe container or serve right away. The ice cream will be soft and creamy. If you like a harder texture, allow the ice cream to freeze for 2 hours or more before serving.

<u>*Without an ice cream maker*</u>

1. In a large saucepan, add the whole milk, heavy cream, and sugar.
2. Over medium-low heat, bring the mixture to a soft simmering and whisk constantly until the sugar is completely dissolved, about 10 to 12 minutes.
3. Pour the mixture in a clean bowl. Stir in the vanilla extract and let cool to room temperature.
4. Pour the mixture in a Pyrex or stainless steel 9x13-inch pan. And place in the freezer for 30 minutes. The edges should start freezing. Using an electric handheld mixer, beat the ice cream on low speed for 1 minute.

5.
6. Return to the freezer for another 30 minutes and beat again as before. Do this same step 4-5 times until the ice cream has hardened. If at any point, the ice cream becomes too hard to beat, place it in the refrigerator until it becomes soft enough to beat.
7. Serve right away or transfer the ice cream to an airtight freezer-safe container.

Nutrition per Serving

Calories 311, fat 14 g, carbs 45 g, sugar 43 g,pProtein 5 g, sodium 69 mg

Coffee Ice Cream

Makes about 4 cups (½ cup per serving)

Ingredients

½ cup hot water
2 tablespoons instant coffee
14 oz. can sweetened condensed milk
1 teaspoon vanilla extract
2 cups cream

Directions

With an ice cream maker

1. Freeze the ice cream maker bowl according to manufacturer instructions, usually 12 to 24 hours.
2. Meanwhile in a mixing bowl, add the hot water and the instant coffee powder and stir until everything is dissolved.
3. Stir in the sweetened condensed milk and vanilla extract and pour in the heavy cream. Whisk to combine.
4. Transfer the mixture into a clean bowl preferably with a spout.
5. Cover the mixture with plastic wrap and let the mixture cool in the refrigerator for at least 2 to 12 hours.
6. Pull out the ice cream mixture from the refrigerator and stir a few times.
7. Install the frozen ice cream maker bowl and pour the mixture into it.
8. Connect the machine and press ice cream and the start button.
9. When the cycle is finished, transfer the ice cream to an airtight freezer-safe container or serve right away. The ice cream will be soft and creamy. If you like a harder texture, allow the ice cream to freeze for 2 hours or more before serving.

Without an ice cream maker

1. In a mixing bowl, add the hot water and the instant coffee powder and stir until everything is dissolved.
2. Stir in the sweetened condensed milk, vanilla extract, and pour in the heavy cream. Whisk to combine.
3. Pour the mixture in a Pyrex or stainless steel 9x13-inch pan. And place in the freezer for 30 minutes. The edges should start freezing. Using an electric handheld mix, beat the ice cream on low speed for 1 minute.
4. Return to the freezer for another 30 minutes and beat again as before. Do this same step 4-5 times until the ice cream has hardened. If at any point, the ice cream is too hard to beat, place it in the refrigerator until it becomes soft enough to beat.
5. Serve right away or transfer the ice cream to an airtight freezer-safe container.

Nutrition per Serving
Calories 311, fat 14 g, carbs 45 g, sugar 43 g, protein 5 g, sodium 69 mg

Chocolate Ice Cream

Makes about 4 cups (½ cup per serving)

Ingredients

3 tablespoons cocoa powder
1 cup sweetened condensed milk
¼ cup sugar
6 egg yolks
1 teaspoon vanilla extract
2 cups cream

Directions

With an ice cream maker

1. Freeze the ice cream maker bowl according to manufacturer instructions, usually 12 to 24 hours.
2. Meanwhile in a large saucepan, heat the cream and warm it up together with the cocoa powder over medium-low heat. Bring the mixture to a soft simmer for about 10 to 12 minutes. Set aside.
3. In a mixing bowl, add the sugar and the egg yolks. Whisk to combine. While stirring constantly, pour in the hot cream slowly to temper the egg yolks.
4. Pour the mixture back into the saucepan and heat again over medium-low heat until creamy and thickened. You know it's ready when the mixture coats the back of a spoon.
5. Pour the mixture in a clean bowl, preferably with a spout, over a fine-mesh sieve to strain and remove any cooked pieces of the egg yolks.
6. In the strained mixture, pour in the condensed milk and vanilla extract. Mix until everything is incorporated.
7. Cover the mixture with plastic wrap and let the mixture cool in the refrigerator for at least 2 to 12 hours.
8. Pull out the ice cream mixture from the refrigerator and stir a few times.
9. Install the frozen ice cream maker bowl and pour the mixture into it.
10. Connect the machine and press ice cream and the start button.
11. When the cycle is finished, transfer the ice cream to an airtight freezer-safe container or serve right away. The ice cream will be soft and creamy. If you like a harder texture, allow the ice cream to freeze for 2 hours or more before serving.

Without an ice cream maker

1. In a large saucepan, heat the cream and warm it up together with the cocoa powder over medium-low heat. Bring the mixture to a soft simmer for about 10 to 12 minutes. Set aside.
2. In a mixing bowl, add the sugar and the egg yolks. Whisk to combine. While stirring constantly, pour in the hot cream slowly to temper the egg yolks.

3. Pour the mixture back into the saucepan and heat again over medium-low heat until creamy and thickened. You know it's ready when the mixture coats the back of a spoon.
4. Pour the mixture in a Pyrex or stainless steel 9x13-inch pan over a fine-mesh sieve to strain and remove any cooked pieces of the egg yolks.
5. In the strained mixture, pour in the condensed milk and vanilla extract. Mix until everything is incorporated and let cool to room temperature.
6. Place in the freezer for 30 minutes. The edges should start freezing. Using an electric handheld mixer, beat the ice cream for 1 minute.
7. Return to the freezer for another 30 minutes and beat again as before. Do this same step 4-5 times until the ice creamhass hardened. If at any point, the ice cream is too hard to beat, place it in the refrigerator until it becomes soft enough to beat.
8. Serve right away or transfer the ice cream to an airtight freezer-safe container.

Nutrition per Serving

Calories 462, fat 21 g, carbs 61 g, sugar 57 g, protein 12 g, sodium 149 mg

Matcha Green Tea Ice Cream

Makes about 4 cups (½ cup per serving)

Ingredients
1 tablespoon matcha green tea powder
2 egg yolks
5 tablespoons granulated sugar
1 teaspoon vanilla extract
1 ½ cups cream

Directions

With an ice cream maker

1. Freeze the ice cream maker bowl according to manufacturer instructions, usually 12 to 24 hours.
2. Meanwhile in a large saucepan, add the cream together with the green tea powder over medium-low heat. Bring the mixture to a soft simmer for about 10 to 12 minutes. Set aside.
3. In a mixing bowl, add the sugar and the egg yolks. Whisk to combine. While stirring constantly, pour in the hot cream slowly to temper the egg yolks.
4. Pour the mixture back into the saucepan and heat the whole mixture again over medium-low heat until creamy and thickened. You know it's ready when the mixture coats the back of a spoon.
5. Pour the mixture into a clean bowl, preferably with a spout, over a fine-mesh sieve to strain and remove any cooked pieces of the egg yolks.
6. In the strained mixture, stir in the vanilla extract.
7. Cover the mixture with plastic wrap and let the mixture cool in the refrigerator for at least 2 to 12 hours.
8. Pull out the ice cream mixture from the refrigerator and stir a few times.
9. Install the frozen ice cream maker bowl and pour the mixture into it.
10. Connect the machine and press ice cream and the start button.
11. When the cycle is finished, transfer the ice cream to an airtight freezer-safe container or serve right away. The ice cream will be soft and creamy. If you like a harder texture, allow the ice cream to freeze for 2 hours or more before serving.

Without an ice cream maker

1. In a large saucepan, add the cream together with the green tea powder over medium-low heat. Bring the mixture to a soft simmer for about 10 to 12 minutes. Set aside.
2. In a mixing bowl, add the sugar and the egg yolks. Whisk to combine. While stirring constantly, pour in the hot cream slowly to temper the egg yolks.

3. Pour the mixture back into the saucepan and heat the whole mixture again over medium-low heat until creamy and thickened. You know it's ready when the mixture coats the back of a spoon.
4. Pour the mixture in a Pyrex or stainless steel 9x13-inch pan over a fine-mesh sieve to strain and remove any cooked pieces of the egg yolks.
5. In the strained mixture, stir in the vanilla extract.
6. Place in the freezer for 30 minutes. The edges should start freezing. Using an electric handheld mixer, beat the ice cream for 1 minute.
7. Return to the freezer for another 30 minutes and beat again as before. Do this same step 4-5 times until the ice cream has hardened. If at any point, the ice cream is too hard to beat, place it in the refrigerator until it becomes soft enough to beat.
8. Serve right away or transfer the ice cream to an airtight freezer-safe container.

Nutrition per Serving

Calories 159, fat 7 g, carbs 18 g, sugar 17 g, Protein 7 g, sodium 33 mg,

Cinnamon Infused Ice Cream

Makes about 4 cups (½ cup per serving)

Ingredients

¾ cup granulated sugar
1 cup heavy whipping cream
2 cups milk
2 teaspoons ground cinnamon
2 teaspoons vanilla extract

Directions

With an ice cream maker

1. Freeze the ice cream maker bowl according to manufacturer instructions, usually 12 to 24 hours.
2. Meanwhile in a saucepan, heat the heavy cream, milk, cinnamon, and sugar over medium-low heat. Bring the mixture to a soft simmer for about 10 to 12 minutes. Stir until the sugar is completely dissolved and set aside.
3. Pour the mixture in a bowl, preferably with a spout, and stir in the vanilla extract. Let cool to room temperature.
4. Cover the mixture with plastic wrap and let the mixture cool in the refrigerator for at least 2 to 12 hours.
5. Pull out the ice cream mixture from the refrigerator and stir a few times.
6. Install the frozen ice cream maker bowl and pour the mixture into it.
7. Connect the machine and press ice cream and the start button.
8. When the cycle is finished, transfer the ice cream to an airtight freezer-safe container or serve right away. The ice cream will be soft and creamy. If you like a harder texture, allow the ice cream to freeze for 2 hours or more before serving.

Without an ice cream maker

1. In a saucepan, heat the heavy cream, milk, cinnamon, and sugar over medium-low heat. Bring the mixture to a soft simmer for about 10 to 12 minutes. Stir until the sugar is completely dissolved and set aside.
2. Stir in the vanilla extract.
3. Pour the mixture in a Pyrex or stainless steel 9x13-inch pan. And place in the freezer for 30 minutes. The edges should start freezing. Using an electric handheld mixer, beat the ice cream for 1 minute.
4. Return to the freezer for another 30 minutes and beat again as before. Do this same step 4-5 times until the ice cream has hardened. If at any point, the ice cream is too hard to beat, place it in the refrigerator until it becomes soft enough to beat.
5. Serve right away or transfer the ice cream to an airtight freezer-safe container.

Nutrition per Serving
Calories 314, fat 14 g, carbs 46 g, sugar 43 g, protein 5 g, sodium 69 mg

Pecan and Maple Syrup Ice Cream

Makes about 4 cups (½ cup per serving)

Ingredients
¾ cup maple syrup
2 cups cream
2 cups whole milk
1 teaspoon vanilla extract
1 cup chopped pecans

Directions
With an ice cream maker

1. Freeze the ice cream maker bowl according to manufacturer instructions, usually 12 to 24 hours.
2. Meanwhile in a large saucepan, heat the cream and milk together with the maple syrup over medium-low heat. Bring the mixture to a soft simmer for about 10 to 12 minutes.
3. Pour the mixture into a clean bowl, preferably with a spout, and stir in the vanilla. Let cool at room temperature.
4. Cover the mixture with plastic wrap and let the mixture cool in the refrigerator for at least 2 to 12 hours.
5. Pull out the ice cream mixture from the refrigerator and stir a few times.
6. Install the frozen ice cream maker bowl and pour the mixture into it.
7. Connect the machine and press ice cream and the start button.
8. About 5-6 minutes before the end of the churning process, add the chopped pecans little by little into the ice cream and let it mix in.
9. When the cycle is finished, transfer the ice cream to an airtight freezer-safe container or serve right away. The ice cream will be soft and creamy. If you like a harder texture, allow the ice cream to freeze for 2 hours or more before serving.

Without an ice cream maker

1. In a large saucepan, heat the cream and milk together with the maple syrup over medium-low heat. Bring the mixture to a soft simmer for about 10 to 12 minutes.
2. Pour the mixture in a Pyrex or stainless steel 9x13-inch pan. Stir in the vanilla and let cool at room temperature. Place in the freezer for 30 minutes. The edges should start freezing. Using an electric handheld mixer, beat the ice cream for 1 minute.
3. Return to the freezer for another 30 minutes and beat again as before. Do this same step 4-5 times until the ice cream has hardened. If at any point, the ice cream is too hard to beat, place it in the refrigerator until it becomes soft enough to beat.

4. In the last churning add the chopped pecans and beat the ice cream one last time, so the pecans will spread evenly.
5. Serve right away or transfer the ice cream to an airtight freezer-safe container.

Nutrition per Serving

Calories 516, fat 32 g, carbs 53 g, sugar 45 g
Protein 8 g, sodium 93 mg

Chocolate and Peanut Butter Ice Cream

Makes about 4 cups (½ cup per serving)

Ingredients

3 tablespoons cocoa powder
1 cup sweetened condensed milk
¼ cup sugar
6 egg yolks
¾ cup peanut butter
1 teaspoon vanilla extract
2 cups cream

Directions

With an ice cream maker

1. Freeze the ice cream maker bowl according to manufacturer instructions, usually 12 to 24 hours.
2. Meanwhile in a large saucepan, add the cream and the cocoa powder over medium-low heat. Bring the mixture to a soft simmer for about 10 to 12 minutes. Set aside.
3. In a mixing bowl, add the sugar and the egg yolks and whisk to combine. While constantly stirring, pour in the hot cream slowly to temper the egg yolks.
4. Pour the mixture back into the saucepan and heat the whole mixture again over medium-low heat until creamy and thickened. You know it's ready when the mixture coats the back of a spoon.
5. Pour the mixture in a clean bowl over a fine-mesh sieve to strain and remove any cooked pieces of the egg yolks.
6. In the strained mixture, pour in the peanut butter, condensed milk, and vanilla extract. Stir until the peanut butter is dissolved into the mixture. Let cool to room temperature.
7. Cover the mixture with plastic wrap and let the mixture cool in the refrigerator for at least 2 to 12 hours.
8. Pull out the ice cream mixture from the refrigerator and stir a few times.
9. Install the frozen ice cream maker bowl and pour the mixture into it.
10. Connect the machine and press ice cream and the start button.
11. When the cycle is finished, transfer the ice cream to an airtight freezer-safe container or serve right away. The ice cream will be soft and creamy. If you like a harder texture, allow the ice cream to freeze for 2 hours or more before serving.

Without an ice cream maker

1. In a large saucepan, add the cream and the cocoa powder over medium-low heat just. Bring the mixture to a soft simmer for about 10 to 12 minutes. Set aside.
2. In a mixing bowl, add the sugar and the egg yolks and whisk to combine. While constantly stirring, pour in the hot cream slowly to temper the egg yolks.

3. Pour the mixture back into the saucepan and heat the whole mixture again over medium-low heat until creamy and thickened. You know it's ready when the mixture coats the back of a spoon.
4. Pour the mixture in a Pyrex or stainless steel 9x13-inch pan over a fine-mesh sieve to strain and remove any cooked pieces of the egg yolks.
5. In the strained mixture, pour in the peanut butter, condensed milk, and vanilla extract. Stir until the peanut butter is dissolved into the mixture. Let cool to room temperature.
6. Place in the freezer for 30 minutes. The edges should start freezing. Using an electric handheld mixer, beat the ice cream for 1 minute.
7. Return to the freezer for another 30 minutes and beat again as before. Do this same step 4-5 times until the ice cream has hardened. If at any point, the ice cream is too hard to beat, place it in the refrigerator until it becomes soft enough to beat.
8. Serve right away or transfer the ice cream to an airtight freezer-safe container.

Nutrition per Serving
Calories 747, fat 45 g, carbs 71 g, sugar 61 g, protein 24 g, sodium 372 mg,

Bubblegum Ice Cream

Makes about 4 cups (½ cup per serving)

Ingredients

2 ½ cups whole milk

1 ½ tsp bubblegum extract

1 ½ cups heavy cream

¾ cups sugar

3 egg yolks

4 drops food coloring (blue or pink)

1 cup gumballs, mixed colors

Directions

<u>*With an ice cream maker*</u>

1. Freeze the ice cream maker bowl according to manufacturer instructions, usually 12 to 24 hours.
2. Meanwhile in a large saucepan, add the milk and bubblegum extract over medium-low heat. Bring the mixture to a soft simmer for about 10 to 12 minutes. Set aside.
3. In a mixing bowl, add the sugar and the egg yolks and whisk to combine. While stirring constantly, pour in the hot milk mixture slowly to temper the egg yolks.
4. Pour the mixture back into the saucepan and heat the whole mixture again over medium-low heat until creamy and thickened. You know it's ready when the mixture coats the back of a spoon.
5. Pour the mixture in a clean bowl, preferably with a spout, over a fine-mesh sieve to strain and remove any cooked pieces of the egg yolks.
6. In the strained mixture, stir in the bubblegum extract.
7. Cover the mixture with plastic wrap and let the mixture cool in the refrigerator for at least 2 to 12 hours.
8. Pull out the ice cream mixture from the refrigerator and stir a few times.
9. Install the frozen ice cream maker bowl and pour the mixture into the ice cream maker.
10. Connect the machine and press ice cream and the start button.
11. When the cycle is finished, transfer the ice cream to an airtight freezer-safe container or serve right away. The ice cream will be soft and creamy. If you like a harder texture, allow the ice cream to freeze for 2 hours or more before serving.

<u>*Without an ice cream maker*</u>

1. In a large saucepan, add the milk and bubblegum extract over medium-low heat. Bring the mixture to a soft simmer for about 10 to 12 minutes. Set aside.
2. In a mixing bowl, add the sugar and the egg yolks and whisk to combine. While stirring constantly, pour in the hot milk mixture slowly to temper the egg yolks.

3. Pour the mixture back into the saucepan and heat the whole mixture again over medium-low heat until creamy and thickened. You know it's ready when the mixture coats the back of a spoon.
4. Pour the mixture into a Pyrex or stainless steel 9x13-inch pan over a fine-mesh sieve to strain and remove any cooked pieces of the egg yolks.
5. In the strained mixture, stir in the bubblegum extract.
6. Place in the freezer for 30 minutes. The edges should start freezing. Using an electric handheld mixer, beat the ice cream for 1 minute.
7. Return to the freezer for another 30 minutes and beat again as before. Do this same step 4-5 times until the ice cream has hardened. If at any point, the ice cream is too hard to beat, place it in the refrigerator until it becomes soft enough to beat.
8. Serve right away or transfer the ice cream to an airtight freezer-safe container.

Nutrition per Serving
Calories 758, fat 68 g, carbs 38 g, sugar 31 g
Protein 9 g, sodium 94 mg

Old Fashioned Vanilla Ice Cream

Makes about 4 cups (½ cup per serving)

Ingredients

2 cups whole milk
4 large egg yolks
3 large eggs
2 cups heavy cream
1 whole vanilla bean (about 6 inches in length)
1 cup granulated sugar
2 tsp pure vanilla extract

Directions

With an ice cream maker

1. Freeze the ice cream maker bowl according to manufacturer instructions, usually 12 to 24 hours.
2. Meanwhile, in a large saucepan, add the cream and the milk over medium-low heat. Bring the mixture to a soft simmer for about 10 to 12 minutes. Set aside.
3. Scrape the seeds out of the vanilla bean and stir it in the cream/milk mixture. Simmer and stir occasionally.
4. Pour the mixture into a clean bowl, preferably with a spout, over a fine-mesh sieve to strain and remove the vanilla bean pod and sediments, discard. Set aside and let cool at room temperature.
5. In a mixing bowl, add the sugar, eggs, and the egg yolks and whisk to combine. While stirring constantly, pour in the hot cream/milk mixture slowly to temper the egg yolks.
6. Pour the mixture back into the saucepan and heat the whole mixture again over medium-low heat until creamy and thickened. You know it's ready when the mixture coats the back of a spoon.
7. Pour the mixture into a clean bowl, preferably with a spout, over a fine-mesh sieve to strain and remove any cooked pieces of the egg yolks. Discard.
8. In the strained mixture, pour in the vanilla extract and mix until combined.
9. Cover the mixture with plastic wrap and let the mixture cool in the refrigerator for at least 2 to 12 hours.
10. Pull out the ice cream mixture from the refrigerator and stir a few times.
11. Install the frozen ice cream maker bowl and pour the mixture into the ice cream maker.
12. Connect the machine and press ice cream and the start button.
13. When the cycle is finished, transfer the ice cream to an airtight freezer-safe container or serve right away. The ice cream will be soft and creamy. If you like a harder texture, allow the ice cream to freeze for 2 hours or more before serving.

Without an ice cream maker

1. In a large saucepan, add the cream and the milk over medium-low heat. Bring the mixture to a soft simmer for about 10 to 12 minutes. Set aside.
2. Scrape the seeds out of the vanilla bean and stir it in the cream/milk mixture. Simmer and stir occasionally.
3. Pour the mixture into a clean bowl, preferably with a spout, over a fine-mesh sieve to strain and remove the vanilla bean pod and sediments, discard. Set aside and let cool at room temperature.
4. In a mixing bowl, add the sugar, eggs, and the egg yolks and whisk to combine. While stirring constantly, pour in the hot cream/milk mixture slowly to temper the egg yolks.
5. Pour the mixture back into the saucepan and heat the whole mixture again over medium-low heat until creamy and thickened. You know it's ready when the mixture coats the back of a spoon.
6. Pour the mixture in a Pyrex or stainless steel 9x13-inch pan over a fine-mesh sieve to strain and remove any cooked pieces of the egg yolks.
7. In the strained mixture, pour in the vanilla extract and mix until combined.
8. Place in the freezer for 30 minutes. The edges should start freezing. Using an electric handheld mixer, beat the ice cream for 1 minute.
9. Return to the freezer for another 30 minutes and beat again as before. Do this same step 4-5 times until the ice cream has hardened. If at any point, the ice cream is too hard to beat, place it in the refrigerator until it becomes soft enough to beat.
10. Serve right away or transfer the ice cream to an airtight freezer-safe container.

Nutrition per Serving

Calories 481, fat 26 g, carbs 59 g, sugar 56 g, protein 8 g, sodium 86 mg

Blueberry Ice Cream

Makes about 4 cups (½ cup per serving)

Ingredients
1 ½ cup blueberries
1 cup granulated sugar
¼ cup lemon juice
2 cups heavy cream
1 cup whole milk
1 teaspoon vanilla extract
6 large egg yolks

Directions

With an ice cream maker

1. Freeze the ice cream maker bowl according to manufacturer instructions, usually 12 to 24 hours.
2. Meanwhile in a large saucepan, add the cream and the milk over medium-low heat. Bring the mixture to a soft simmer for about 10 to 12 minutes. Set aside.
3. In a mixing bowl, add the sugar and the egg yolks and whisk to combine. While stirring constantly, pour in the hot cream mixture slowly to temper the egg yolks.
4. Pour the mixture back into the saucepan and heat the whole mixture again over medium-low heat until creamy and thickened. You know it's ready when the mixture coats the back of a spoon.
5. Pour the mixture in a clean bowl over a fine-mesh sieve to strain and remove any cooked pieces of the egg yolks.
6. In the strained mixture, pour in the vanilla extract and lemon juice and mix until combined. Let cool at room temperature.
7. Cover the mixture with plastic wrap and let the mixture cool in the refrigerator for at least 2 to 12 hours.
8. Pull out the ice cream mixture from the refrigerator and stir a few times.
9. Install the frozen ice cream maker bowl and pour the mixture into it.
10. Connect the machine and press ice cream and the start button.
11. About 5 minutes before the end of the churning process, add the blueberries little by little into the ice cream and let it mix in.
12. When the cycle is finished, transfer the ice cream to an airtight freezer-safe container or serve right away. The ice cream will be soft and creamy. If you like a harder texture, allow the ice cream to freeze for 2 hours or more before serving.

Without an ice cream maker

1. In a large saucepan, add the cream and the milk over medium-low heat. Bring the mixture to a soft simmer for about 10 to 12 minutes. Set aside.

2. In a mixing bowl, add the sugar and the egg yolks and whisk to combine. While stirring constantly, pour in the hot cream mixture slowly to temper the egg yolks.
3. Pour the mixture back into the saucepan and heat the whole mixture again over medium-low heat until creamy and thickened. You know it's ready when the mixture coats the back of a spoon.
4. Pour the mixture in a Pyrex or stainless steel 9x13-inch pan over a fine-mesh sieve to strain and remove any cooked pieces of the egg yolks.
5. In the strained mixture, pour in the vanilla extract and lemon juice and mix until combined.
6. Place in the freezer for 30 minutes. The edges should start freezing. Using an electric handheld mixer, beat the ice cream for 1 minute.
7. Return to the freezer for another 30 minutes and beat again as before. Do this same step 4-5 times until the ice cream has hardened. If at any point, the ice cream is too hard to beat, place it in the refrigerator until it becomes soft enough to beat.
8. In the last churning, add the blueberries and beat the ice cream one last time, so the blueberries will spread.
9. Serve right away or transfer the ice cream to an airtight freezer-safe container.

Nutrition per Serving

Calories 550, fat 31 g, carbs 64 g, sugar 59 g, protein 8 g, sodium 63 mg

Peach Ice Cream

Makes about 4 cups (½ cup per serving)

Ingredients
1 pound fresh peaches, diced in smaller cubes
¾ cup fine sugar
5 egg yolks
1 ½ cup heavy cream
1 teaspoon vanilla extract

Directions
With an ice cream maker

1. Freeze the ice cream maker bowl according to manufacturer instructions, usually 12 to 24 hours.
2. Meanwhile in a large saucepan, add the cream over medium-low heat. Bring the mixture to a soft simmer for about 10 to 12 minutes. Set aside.
3. In a mixing bowl, add the sugar and the egg yolks and whisk to combine. While stirring constantly, pour in the hot cream mixture slowly to temper the egg yolks.
4. Pour the mixture back into the saucepan and heat the whole mixture again over medium-low heat until creamy and thickened. You know it's ready when the mixture coats the back of a spoon.
5. Pour the mixture in a clean bowl over a fine-mesh sieve to strain and remove any cooked pieces of the egg yolks.
6. In the strained mixture, pour in the vanilla extract and mix until everything is combined. Let cool at room temperature.
7. Cover the mixture with plastic wrap and let the mixture cool in the refrigerator for at least 2 to 12 hours.
8. Pull out the ice cream mixture from the refrigerator and stir a few times.
9. Install the frozen ice cream maker bowl and pour the mixture into the ice cream maker.
10. Connect the machine and press ice cream and the start button.
13. About 5 to 6 minutes before the end of the churning process, add the chopped peaches pieces little by little into the ice cream and let it mix in.
11. When the cycle is finished, transfer the ice cream to an airtight freezer-safe container or serve right away. The ice cream will be soft and creamy. If you like a harder texture, allow the ice cream to freeze for 2 hours or more before serving.

Without an ice cream maker

1. In a large saucepan, add the cream over medium-low heat. Bring the mixture to a soft simmer for about 10 to 12 minutes. Set aside.
2. In a mixing bowl, add the sugar and the egg yolks and whisk to combine. While stirring constantly, pour in the hot cream mixture slowly to temper the egg yolks.

3. Pour the mixture back into the saucepan and heat the whole mixture again over medium-low heat until creamy and thickened. You know it's ready when the mixture coats the back of a spoon.
4. Pour the mixture in a Pyrex or stainless steel 9x13-inch pan over a fine-mesh sieve to strain and remove any cooked pieces of the egg yolks.
5. In the strained mixture, pour in the vanilla extract and mix until everything is combined. Let cool at room temperature.
6. Place in the freezer for 30 minutes. The edges should start freezing. Using an electric handheld mixer, beat the ice cream for 1 minute.
7. Return to the freezer for another 30 minutes and beat again as before. Do this same step 4-5 times until the ice cream has hardened. If at any point, the ice cream is too hard to beat, place it in the refrigerator until it becomes soft enough to beat.
8. In the last churning add the diced peach pieces and beat the ice cream one last time, so the peaches will spread.
9. Serve right away or transfer the ice cream to an airtight freezer-safe container.

Nutrition per Serving

Calories 381, fat 22 g, carbs 43 g, sugar 41 g, protein 5 g, sodium 27 mg

Pistachio Ice Cream

Makes about 4 cups (½ cup per serving)

Ingredients

1 cup whole milk
2 cups heavy cream
¾ cup honey
1 teaspoon vanilla extract
1 cup crushed pistachios

Directions

With an ice cream maker

1. Freeze the ice cream maker bowl according to manufacturer instructions, usually 12 to 24 hours.
2. Meanwhile in a large saucepan, add the cream, milk, and honey over medium-low heat. Bring the mixture to a soft simmer for about 10 to 12 minutes. Set aside.
3. Stir in the vanilla extract.
4. Pour the mixture into a clean bowl, preferably with a spout, and let it cool at room temperature.
5. Cover the mixture with plastic wrap and let the mixture cool in the refrigerator for at least 2 to 12 hours.
6. Pull out the ice cream mixture from the refrigerator and stir a few times.
7. Install the frozen ice cream maker bowl and pour the mixture into the ice cream maker.
8. Connect the machine and press ice cream and the start button.
9. About 5 minutes before the end of the churning process, add the chopped pistachios little by little into the ice cream and let it mix in.
10. When the cycle is finished, transfer the ice cream to an airtight freezer-safe container or serve right away. The ice cream will be soft and creamy. If you like a harder texture, allow the ice cream to freeze for 2 hours or more before serving.

Without an ice cream maker

1. In a large saucepan, add the cream, milk, and honey over medium-low heat. Bring the mixture to a soft simmer for about 10 to 12 minutes. Set aside.
2. Stir in the vanilla extract.
3. Pour the mixture in a Pyrex or stainless steel 9x13-inch pan and let it cool to room temperature.
4. When the mixture is cold enough, place it in the freezer for 30 minutes. The edges should start freezing. Using an electric handheld mixer, beat the ice cream for 1 minute.

5. Return to the freezer for another 30 minutes and beat again as before. Do this same step 4-5 times until the ice cream has hardened. If at any point, the ice cream is too hard to beat, place it in the refrigerator until it becomes soft enough to beat.
6. In the last churning add the chopped pistachios and beat the ice cream one last time, so the pistachios will spread.
7. Serve right away or transfer the ice cream to an airtight freezer-safe container.

Nutrition per Serving

Calories 515, fat 30 g, carbs 61 g, sugar 56 g
Protein 7 g, sodium 137 mg

Hazelnut Ice Cream

Makes about 4 cups (½ cup per serving)

Ingredients

1 cup whole milk
2 cups heavy cream
¾ cup powdered sugar
2 teaspoons vanilla extract
2 cups crushed hazelnuts

Directions

With an ice cream maker

1. Freeze the ice cream maker bowl according to manufacturer instructions, usually 12 to 24 hours.
2. Meanwhile in a large mixing bowl, add the cream, milk, and powdered sugar and whisk until completely incorporated.
3. Stir in the vanilla extract.
4. Cover the mixture with plastic wrap and let the mixture cool in the refrigerator for at least 2 to 12 hours.
5. Pull out the ice cream mixture from the refrigerator and stir it a few times.
6. Install the frozen ice cream maker bowl and pour the mixture into it.
7. Connect the machine and press ice cream and the start button.
8. About 5 to 6 minutes before the end of the churning process, add the crushed hazelnuts little by little into the ice cream and let it mix in.
9. When the cycle is finished, transfer the ice cream to an airtight freezer-safe container or serve right away. The ice cream will be soft and creamy. If you like a harder texture, allow the ice cream to freeze for 2 hours or more before serving.

Without an ice cream maker

1. In a large mixing bowl, add the cream, milk, and powdered sugar and whisk until completely incorporated.
2. Stir in the vanilla extract.
3. Pour the mixture in a Pyrex or stainless steel 9x13-inch pan. And place in the freezer for 30 minutes. The edges should start freezing. Using an electric handheld mixer, beat the ice cream for 1 minute.
4. Return to the freezer for another 30 minutes and beat again as before. Do this same step 4-5 times until the ice cream has hardened. If at any point, the ice cream is too hard to beat, place it in the refrigerator until it becomes soft enough to beat.
5. In the last churning add the crushed hazelnuts and beat the ice cream one last time, so the hazelnuts will spread.
6. Serve right away or transfer the ice cream to an airtight freezer-safe container.

Nutrition per Serving
Calories 573, fat 47 g, carbs 33.4 g, sugar 27 g
Protein 9 g, sodium 48 mg

Hazelnut and Chocolate Ice Cream

Makes about 4 cups (½ cup per serving)

Ingredients

1 cup whole milk
4 tablespoons cocoa powder
2 cups heavy cream
¾ cup powdered sugar
2 teaspoons vanilla extract
1 ½ cups crushed hazelnuts

Directions

With an ice cream maker

1. Freeze the ice cream maker bowl according to manufacturer instructions, usually 12 to 24 hours.
2. Meanwhile in a large saucepan, add the cream, milk, cocoa powder, and powdered sugar over medium heat. Bring the mixture to a soft simmer for about 10 to 12 minutes. Set aside.
3. Stir in the vanilla extract.
4. Pour the mixture in a clean bowl and let it cool to room temperature.
5. Cover the mixture with plastic wrap and let the mixture cool in the refrigerator for at least 2 to 12 hours.
6. Pull out the ice cream mixture from the refrigerator and whisk to mix it well.
7. Install the frozen ice cream maker bowl and pour the mixture into the ice cream maker.
8. Connect the machine and press ice cream and the start button.
9. About 5 minutes before the end of the churning process, add the chopped hazelnuts little by little into the ice cream and let it mix in.
10. When the cycle is finished, transfer the ice cream to an airtight freezer-safe container or serve right away. The ice cream will be soft and creamy. If you like a harder texture, allow the ice cream to freeze for 2 hours or more before serving.

Without an ice cream maker

1. In a large saucepan, add the cream, milk, cocoa powder, and powdered sugar over medium heat. Bring the mixture to a soft simmer for about 10 to 12 minutes. Set aside.
2. Stir in the vanilla extract.
3. Pour the mixture in a Pyrex or stainless steel 9x13-inch pan and let it cool to room temperature.
4. When the mixture is cold enough, place it in the freezer for 30 minutes. The edges should start freezing. Using an electric handheld mixer, beat the ice cream for 1 minute.

5. Return to the freezer for another 30 minutes and beat again as before. Do this same step 4-5 times until the ice cream has hardened. If at any point, the ice cream is too hard to beat, place it in the refrigerator until it becomes soft enough to beat.
6. In the last churning add the chopped hazelnuts and beat the ice cream one last time, so the hazelnuts will spread.
7. Serve right away or transfer the ice cream to an airtight freezer-safe container.

Nutrition per Serving
Calories 526, fat 42 g, carbs 35 g, sugar 27 g
Protein 8 g, sodium 49 mg

Blackberry Ice Cream

Makes about 4 cups (½ cup per serving)

Ingredients

2 cups blackberries
1 cup granulated sugar
juice of 1 lemon
1 ½ cups heavy cream
½ cup sour cream

Directions

With an ice cream maker

1. Freeze the ice cream maker bowl according to manufacturer instructions, usually 12 to 24 hours.
2. Meanwhile in a large mixing bowl, add the sugar and the lemon juice, whisk to combine.
3. Add the heavy cream and sour cream and whisk again until the mixture is completely incorporated.
4. Cover the mixture with plastic wrap and let the mixture cool in the refrigerator for at least 2 to 12 hours.
5. Pull out the ice cream mixture from the refrigerator and stir a few times.
6. Install the frozen ice cream maker bowl and pour the mixture into the ice cream maker.
7. Connect the machine and press ice cream and the start button.
8. About 5 minutes before the end of the churning process, add the blackberries little by little into the ice cream and let it mix in.
9. When the cycle is finished, transfer the ice cream to an airtight freezer-safe container or serve right away. The ice cream will be soft and creamy. If you like a harder texture, allow the ice cream to freeze for 2 hours or more before serving.

Without an ice cream maker

1. In a large mixing bowl, add the sugar and the lemon juice, whisk to combine.
2. Add the heavy cream and sour cream and whisk again until the mixture is completely incorporated.
3. Pour the mixture in a Pyrex or stainless steel 9x13-inch pan and place it in the freezer for 30 minutes. The edges should start freezing. Using an electric handheld mixer, beat the ice cream for 1 minute.
4. Return to the freezer for another 30 minutes and beat again as before. Do this same step 4-5 times until the ice cream has hardened. If at any point, the ice cream is too hard to beat, place it in the refrigerator until it becomes soft enough to beat.

5. In the last churning add the blackberries and beat the ice cream one last time, so the blackberries will spread.
6. Serve right away or transfer the ice cream to an airtight freezer-safe container.

Nutrition per Serving
Calories 439, fat 23 g, carbs 61 g, sugar 55 g
Protein 3 g, sodium 33 mg

Mango and Coconut Milk Ice Cream

Makes about 4 cups (½ cup per serving)

Ingredients

3 cups mango, peeled and cut into cubes
¼ cup whole milk
¾ cup powdered sugar
1 ½ cups heavy cream
½ cup coconut milk

Directions

With an ice cream maker

1. Freeze the ice cream maker bowl according to manufacturer instructions, usually 12 to 24 hours.
2. Meanwhile in a large mixing bowl, add the milk, powdered sugar, heavy cream, and coconut milk.
3. Mix until everything is combined.
4. Cover the mixture with plastic wrap and let the mixture cool in the refrigerator for at least 2 to 12 hours.
5. Pull out the ice cream mixture from the refrigerator and stir a few times.
6. Install the frozen ice cream maker bowl and pour the mixture into it.
7. Connect the machine and press ice cream and the start button.
8. About 5 to 6 minutes before the end of the churning process, add the diced mango pieces little by little into the ice cream and let it mix in.
9. When the cycle is finished, transfer the ice cream to an airtight freezer-safe container or serve right away. The ice cream will be soft and creamy. If you like a harder texture, allow the ice cream to freeze for 2 hours or more before serving.

Without an ice cream maker

1. In a large mixing bowl, add the milk, powdered sugar, heavy cream, and coconut milk.
2. Mix until everything is combined.
3. Pour the mixture in a Pyrex or stainless steel 9x13-inch pan. And place in the freezer for 30 minutes. The edges should start freezing. Using an electric handheld mixer, beat the ice cream for 1 minute.
4. Return to the freezer for another 30 minutes and beat again as before. Do this same step 4-5 times until the ice cream has hardened. If at any point, the ice cream is too hard to beat, place it in the refrigerator until it becomes soft enough to beat.
5. In the last churning add the diced mango pieces and beat the ice cream one last time, so the mango pieces will spread.
6. Serve right away or transfer the ice cream to an airtight freezer-safe container.

Nutrition per Serving
Calories 395, fat 25 g, carbs 45 g, sugar 41 g, Protein 3 g, sodium 29 mg

Avocado and Mint Ice Cream

Makes about 4 cups (½ cup per serving)

Ingredients
3 avocados, peeled, cored, and diced
3 tablespoons chopped mint
¾ cup whole milk
2 teaspoons vanilla extract
¾ cup powdered sugar
1 ½ cups heavy cream

Directions
With an ice cream maker

1. Freeze the ice cream maker bowl according to manufacturer instructions, usually 12 to 24 hours.
2. Meanwhile in a high-speed blender, add the avocado, chopped mint, and powdered sugar.
3. Blitz until you get a smooth and creamy mixture it will take about 3 minutes.
4. Pour the mixture in a clean bowl, preferably with a spout, and stir in the vanilla extract and heavy cream. Mix until combined.
5. Cover the mixture with plastic wrap and let the mixture cool in the refrigerator for at least 2 to 12hours.
6. Pull out the ice cream mixture from the refrigerator and stir it a few times.
7. Install the frozen ice cream maker bowl and pour the mixture into it.
8. Connect the machine and press ice cream and the start button.
9. When the cycle is finished, transfer the ice cream to an airtight freezer-safe container or serve right away. The ice cream will be soft and creamy. If you like a harder texture, allow the ice cream to freeze for 2 hours or more before serving.

Without an ice cream maker

1. In a high-speed blender, add the avocado, chopped mint, and powdered sugar.
2. Blitz until you get a smooth and creamy mixture it will take about 3 minutes.
3. Pour the mixture in a Pyrex or stainless steel 9x13-inch pan and stir in the vanilla extract and heavy cream. Mix until combined.
4. Place it in the freezer for 30 minutes. The edges should start freezing. Using an electric handheld mixer, beat the ice cream for 1 minute.
5. Return to the freezer for another 30 minutes and beat again as before. Do this same step 4-5 times until the ice cream has hardened. If at any point, the ice cream is too hard to beat, place it in the refrigerator until it becomes soft enough to beat.
6. Serve right away or transfer the ice cream to an airtight freezer-safe container.

Nutrition per Serving
Calories 586, fat 48 g, carbs 39 g, sugar 26 g
Protein 5 g, sodium 46 mg

Papaya and Passion Fruit Ice Cream

Makes about 4 cups (½ cup per serving)

Ingredients

3 cups papaya, peeled and diced into cubes
¾ cup whole milk
3 passion fruits, pulp out
1 teaspoons vanilla extract
¾ cup powdered sugar
2 cups heavy cream

Directions

With an ice cream maker

1. Freeze the ice cream maker bowl according to manufacturer instructions, usually 12 to 24 hours.
2. Meanwhile in a high-speed blender, add the papaya, milk, passion fruit pulp, and powdered sugar.
3. Blitz until you get a smooth and combined mixture, it will take about 3 minutes.
4. Pour the mixture in a clean bowl, preferably with a spout and stir in the vanilla extract and heavy cream. Mix until combined.
5. Cover the mixture with plastic wrap and let the mixture cool in the refrigerator for at least 2 to 12 hours.
6. Pull out the ice cream mixture from the refrigerator and stir a few times.
7. Install the frozen ice cream maker bowl and pour the mixture into it.
8. Connect the machine and press ice cream and the start button.
9. When the cycle is finished, transfer the ice cream to an airtight freezer-safe container or serve right away. The ice cream will be soft and creamy. If you like a harder texture, allow the ice cream to freeze for 2 hours or more before serving.

Without an ice cream maker

1. In a high-speed blender, add the papaya, milk, passion fruit pulp, and powdered sugar.
2. Blitz until you get a smooth and combined mixture, it will take about 3 minutes.
3. Pour the mixture in a Pyrex or stainless steel 9x13-inch pan and stir in the vanilla extract and heavy cream. Mix until combined.
4. Place it in the freezer for 30 minutes. The edges should start freezing. Using an electric handheld mixer, beat the ice cream for 1 minute.
5. Return to the freezer for another 30 minutes and beat again as before. Do this same step 4-5 times until the ice cream has hardened. If at any point, the ice cream is too hard to beat, place it in the refrigerator until it becomes soft enough to beat.
6. Serve right away or transfer the ice cream to an airtight freezer-safe container.

Nutrition per Serving

Calories 385, fat 24 g, carbs 41 g, sugar 35 g
Protein 4 g, sodium 54 mg

Salted Caramel Ice Cream

Makes about 4 cups (½ cup per serving)

Ingredients

1 ¼ cup sugar
1 cup heavy cream
½ teaspoon salt
1 teaspoon vanilla extract
1 cup whole milk
1 ½ cup cream

Directions

With an ice cream maker

1. Freeze the ice cream maker bowl according to manufacturer instructions, usually 12 to 24 hours.
2. Meanwhile, in a saucepan, warm the sugar over medium heat until melted and amber color develops.
3. Stir in the heavy cream and simmer for 5 minutes. Set aside.
4. Stir in the salt and let it cool completely.
5. In a mixing bowl, add the whole milk and pour caramel mixture, whisk until well incorporated.
6. Cover the mixture with plastic wrap and let the mixture cool in the refrigerator for at least 2 to 12 hours.
7. Pull out the ice cream mixture from the refrigerator and stir a few times.
8. Install the frozen ice cream maker bowl and pour the mixture into it.
9. Connect the machine and press ice cream and the start button.
10. When the cycle is finished, transfer the ice cream to an airtight freezer-safe container or serve right away. The ice cream will be soft and creamy. If you like a harder texture, allow the ice cream to freeze for 2 hours or more before serving.

Without an ice cream maker

1. In a saucepan, warm the sugar over medium heat until melted and amber color develops.
2. Stir in the heavy cream and simmer for 5 minutes. Set aside.
3. Stir in the salt and let it cool completely.
4. In a mixing bowl, add the whole milk and pour caramel mixture, whisk until well incorporated.
5. Pour the mixture in a Pyrex or stainless steel 9x13-inch pan. And place in the freezer for 30 minutes. The edges should start freezing. Using an electric handheld mixer, beat the ice cream for 1 minute

6. Return to the freezer for another 30 minutes and beat again as before. Do this same step 4-5 times until the ice cream has hardened. If at any point, the ice cream is too hard to beat, place it in the refrigerator until it becomes soft enough to beat.
7. Serve right away or transfer the ice cream to an airtight freezer-safe container.

Nutrition per Serving

Calories 435, fat 18 g, carbs 69 g, sugar 68 g
Protein 3 g, sodium 356 mg

Strawberry and Coconut Ice Cream

Makes about 4 cups (½ cup per serving)

Ingredients

3 cups strawberries, cut in halves
1 cup whole milk
¾ cup powdered sugar
1 teaspoon vanilla extract
1 ½ cups heavy cream
½ cup coconut milk

Directions

With an ice cream maker

1. Freeze the ice cream maker bowl according to manufacturer instructions, usually 12 to 24 hours.
2. In a high-speed blender, add the strawberries, milk, and powdered sugar.
3. Blitz until you get a smooth and creamy mixture. Blend for about 3 minutes.
4. Pour the mixture in a bowl and stir in the vanilla extract, coconut milk, and heavy cream. Mix until combined.
5. Cover the mixture with plastic wrap and let the mixture cool in the refrigerator for at least 2 to 12 hours.
6. Pull out the ice cream mixture from the refrigerator and stir a few times.
7. Install the frozen ice cream maker bowl and pour the mixture into the ice cream maker.
8. Connect the machine and press ice cream and the start button.
9. When the cycle is finished, transfer the ice cream to an airtight freezer-safe container or serve right away. The ice cream will be soft and creamy. If you like a harder texture, allow the ice cream to freeze for 2 hours or more before serving.

Without an ice cream maker

1. In a high-speed blender, add the strawberries, milk, and powdered sugar.
2. Blitz until you get a smooth and creamy mixture. Blend for about 3 minutes.
3. Pour the mixture in a Pyrex or stainless steel 9x13-inch pan and stir in the vanilla extract, coconut milk, and heavy cream. Mix until combined.
4. Place it in the freezer for 30 minutes. The edges should start freezing. Using an electric handheld mixer, beat the ice cream for 1 minute.
5. Return to the freezer for another 30 minutes and beat again as before. Do this same step 4-5 times until the ice cream has hardened. If at any point, the ice cream is too hard to beat, place it in the refrigerator until it becomes soft enough to beat.
6. Serve right away or transfer the ice cream to an airtight freezer-safe container.

Nutrition per Serving
Calories 386, fat 26 g, carbs 37 g, sugar 32 g
Protein 4 g, sodium 47 mg

Almond Coconut Ice Cream

Makes about 4 cups (½ cup per serving)

Ingredients

1 cup whole milk
2 cups heavy cream
¾ cup powdered sugar
2 teaspoons vanilla extract
¼ cup crushed almonds
½ cup coconut flakes

Directions

With an ice cream maker

1. Freeze the ice cream maker bowl according to manufacturer instructions, usually 12 to 24 hours.
2. Meanwhile in a large mixing bowl, add the milk, heavy cream, and powdered sugar.
3. Add the vanilla extract and mix until everything is combined.
4. Cover the mixture with plastic wrap and let the mixture cool in the refrigerator for at least 2 to 12 hours.
5. Pull out the ice cream mixture from the refrigerator and stir a few times.
6. Install the frozen ice cream maker bowl and pour the mixture into it.
7. Connect the machine and press ice cream and the start button.
8. About 5 minutes before the end of the churning process, add the crushed almonds and coconut little by little into the ice cream and let it mix in.
9. When the cycle is finished, transfer the ice cream to an airtight freezer-safe container or serve right away. The ice cream will be soft and creamy. If you like a harder texture, allow the ice cream to freeze for 2 hours or more before serving.

Without an ice cream maker

1. In a large mixing bowl, add the milk, heavy cream and powdered sugar.
2. Add the vanilla extract and mix until everything is combined.
3. Pour the mixture in a Pyrex or stainless steel 9x13-inch pan. And place in the freezer for 30 minutes. The edges should start freezing. Using an electric handheld mixer, beat the ice cream for 1 minute.
4. Return to the freezer for another 30 minutes and beat again as before. Do this same step 4-5 times until the ice cream has hardened. If at any point, the ice cream is too hard to beat, place it in the refrigerator until it becomes soft enough to beat.
5. In the last churning add the crushed almonds and beat the ice cream one last time, so the almonds will spread.
6. Serve right away or transfer the ice cream to an airtight freezer-safe container.

Nutrition per Serving
Calories 612, fat 48 g, carbs 37 g, sugar 28 g
Protein 13 g, sodium 48 mg

Almond Butter Ice Cream

Makes about 4 cups (½ cup per serving)

Ingredients

1 cup whole milk
2 cups heavy cream
½ cup powdered sugar
2 teaspoons vanilla extract
1 cup almond butter

Directions

With an ice cream maker

1. Freeze the ice cream maker bowl according to manufacturer instructions, usually 12 to 24 hours.
2. Meanwhile in a large saucepan, add the milk, heavy cream, powdered sugar over medium heat. Bring the mixture to a soft simmer for about 10 to 12 minutes. Set aside.
3. Stir in the vanilla extract and almond butter. Mix until everything is combined and the almond butter is melted. It will take around 2 minutes.
4. Pour the mixture in a clean bowl, preferably with a spout, and let it cool at room temperature.
5. Cover the mixture with plastic wrap and let the mixture cool in the refrigerator for at least 2 to 12 hours.
6. Pull out the ice cream mixture from the refrigerator and stir a few times.
7. Install the frozen ice cream maker bowl and pour the mixture into the ice cream maker.
8. Connect the machine and press ice cream and the start button.
9. When the cycle is finished, transfer the ice cream to an airtight freezer-safe container or serve right away. The ice cream will be soft and creamy. If you like a harder texture, allow the ice cream to freeze for 2 hours or more before serving.

Without an ice cream maker

1. In a large saucepan, add the milk, heavy cream, powdered sugar over medium heat. Bring the mixture to a soft simmer for about 10 to 12 minutes. Set aside.
2. Stir in the vanilla extract and almond butter. Mix until everything is combined and the almond butter is melted. It will take around 2 minutes.
3. Pour the mixture in a Pyrex or stainless steel 9x13-inch pan and let it cool at room temperature.
4. Place it in the freezer for 30 minutes. The edges should start freezing. Using an electric handheld mixer, beat the ice cream for 1 minute.

5. Return to the freezer for another 30 minutes and beat again as before. Do this same step 4-5 times until the ice cream has hardened. If at any point, the ice cream is too hard to beat, place it in the refrigerator until it becomes soft enough to beat.
6. Serve right away or transfer the ice cream to an airtight freezer-safe container.

Nutrition per Serving

Calories 333, fat 27 g, carbs 20 g, sugar 18 g
Protein 4 g, sodium 48 mg

Rum and Raisin Ice Cream

Makes about 4 cups (½ cup per serving)

Ingredients

¼ cup dark rum
¾ cup powdered sugar
1 teaspoon vanilla extract
1 cup whole milk
2 cups heavy cream
½ cup raisin

Directions

<u>With an ice cream maker</u>

1. Freeze the ice cream maker bowl according to manufacturer instructions, usually 12 to 24 hours.
2. In a large mixing bowl, add the dark rum, powdered sugar, vanilla extract, whole milk, and heavy cream.
3. Mix until everything is combined.
4. Cover the mixture with plastic wrap and let the mixture cool in the refrigerator for at least 2 to 12 hours.
5. Pull out the ice cream mixture from the refrigerator and stir a few times.
6. Install the frozen ice cream maker bowl and pour the mixture into it.
7. Connect the machine and press ice cream and the start button.
8. About 5 to 6 minutes before the cycle ends, add the raisins, a little at a time, so they spread evenly in the ice cream.
9. When the cycle is finished, transfer the ice cream to an airtight freezer-safe container or serve right away. The ice cream will be soft and creamy. If you like a harder texture, allow the ice cream to freeze for 2 hours or more before serving.

<u>Without an ice cream maker</u>

1. In a large mixing bowl, add the dark rum, powdered sugar, vanilla extract, whole milk, and heavy cream.
2. Mix until everything is combined.
4. Pour the mixture in a Pyrex or stainless steel 9x13-inch pan. And place in the freezer for 30 minutes. The edges should start freezing. Using an electric handheld mixer, beat the ice cream for 1 minute.
5. Return to the freezer for another 30 minutes and beat again as before. Do this same step 4-5 times until the ice cream has hardened. If at any point, the ice cream is too hard to beat, place it in the refrigerator until it becomes soft enough to beat.
6. In the last time that you beat the ice cream, add the raisins and beat so the raisins spread evenly in the ice cream.
7. Serve right away or transfer the ice cream to an airtight freezer-safe container.

Nutrition per Serving
Calories 366, fat 24 g, carbs 27 g, sugar 25 g
Protein 3 g, sodium 48 mg

Cookie'n Cream Ice Cream

Makes about 4 cups (½ cup per serving)

Ingredients

1 cup whole milk

2 cups heavy cream

¾ cup granulated sugar

1 teaspoon vanilla extract

16 chocolate sandwich cookies like Oreo cookies, crushed

Directions

With an ice cream maker

1. Freeze the ice cream maker bowl according to manufacturer instructions, usually 12 to 24 hours.
2. Meanwhile in a large saucepan, add the cream, milk, and sugar over medium heat. Bring the mixture to a soft simmer for about 10 to 12 minutes. Set aside.
3. Pour the mixture in a bowl and stir in the vanilla extract.
4. Let it cool at room temperature.
5. Cover the mixture with plastic wrap and let the mixture cool in the refrigerator for at least 2 to 12 hours.
6. Pull out the ice cream mixture from the refrigerator and stir a few times.
7. Install the frozen ice cream maker bowl and pour the mixture into the ice cream maker.
8. Connect the machine and press ice cream and the start button.
9. About 5 minutes before the end of the churning process, add the crushed Oreos little by little into the ice cream and let it mix in.
10. When the cycle is finished, transfer the ice cream to an airtight freezer-safe container or serve right away. The ice cream will be soft and creamy. If you like a harder texture, allow the ice cream to freeze for 2 hours or more before serving.

Without an ice cream maker

1. In a large saucepan, add the cream, milk, and sugar over medium heat. Bring the mixture to a soft simmer for about 10 to 12 minutes. Set aside.
2. Pour the mixture in a Pyrex or stainless steel 9x13-inch pan and stir in the vanilla extract. Bring the mixture to a soft simmer for about 10 to 12 minutes. Set aside.
3. Let it cool at room temperature.
4. When the mixture is cold enough, place it in the freezer for 30 minutes. The edges should start freezing. Using an electric handheld mixer, beat the ice cream for 1 minute.
5. Return to the freezer for another 30 minutes and beat again as before. Do this same step 4-5 times until the ice cream has hardened. If at any point, the ice cream is too hard to beat, place it in the refrigerator until it becomes soft enough to beat.

6. In the last churning add the crushed Oreos and beat the ice cream one last time, so the Oreos will spread.
7. Serve right away or transfer the ice cream to an airtight freezer-safe container.

Nutrition per Serving
Calories 574, fat 32 g, carbs 71 g, sugar 57 g
Protein 5 g, sodium 240 mg

Graham Crackers and Honey Ice Cream

Makes about 4 cups (½ cup per serving)

Ingredients
1 cup whole milk
2 cups heavy cream
½ cup honey
1 teaspoon vanilla extract
7 oz crushed honey graham crackers

Directions
With an ice cream maker

1. Freeze the ice cream maker bowl according to manufacturer instructions, usually 12 to 24 hours.
2. Meanwhile in a large saucepan, add the cream, milk, and honey over medium heat. Bring the mixture to a soft simmer for about 10 to 12 minutes. Set aside.
3. Stir in the vanilla extract.
4. Pour the mixture in a clean bowl, preferably with a spout, and let it cool at room temperature.
5. Cover the mixture with plastic wrap and let the mixture cool in the refrigerator for at least 2 to 12 hours.
6. Pull out the ice cream mixture from the refrigerator and stir a few times.
7. Install the frozen ice cream maker bowl and pour the mixture into the ice cream maker.
8. Connect the machine and press ice cream and the start button.
9. About 5 minutes before the end of the churning process, add the crushed graham crackers by little into the ice cream and let it mix in.
10. When the cycle is finished, transfer the ice cream to an airtight freezer-safe container or serve right away. The ice cream will be soft and creamy. If you like a harder texture, allow the ice cream to freeze for 2 hours or more before serving.

Without an ice cream maker

1. In a large saucepan, add the cream, milk, and honey over medium heat. Bring the mixture to a soft simmer for about 10 to 12 minutes. Set aside.
2. Stir in the vanilla extract.
3. Pour the mixture in a Pyrex or stainless steel 9x13-inch pan and let it cool at room temperature.
4. Place it in the freezer for 30 minutes. The edges should start freezing. Using an electric handheld mixer, beat the ice cream for 1 minute.
5. Return to the freezer for another 30 minutes and beat again as before. Do this same step 4-5 times until the ice cream has hardened. If at any point, the ice cream is too hard to beat, place it in the refrigerator until it becomes soft enough to beat.

6. In the last churning add the crushed graham crackers and beat the ice cream one last time, so the graham crackers will spread.
7. Serve right away or transfer the ice cream to an airtight freezer-safe container.

Nutrition per Serving

Calories 585, fat 29 g, carbs 78 g, sugar 54 g
Protein 7 g, sodium 349 mg

Maple and Walnut Ice Cream

Makes about 4 cups (½ cup per serving)

Ingredients

1 cup walnuts, chopped coarsely
1 ½ cups whole milk
2 ½ cups heavy cream
½ cup maple syrup
1 teaspoon pure vanilla extract

Directions

With an ice cream maker

1. Freeze the ice cream maker bowl according to manufacturer instructions, usually 12 to 24 hours.
2. Meanwhile, add the maple syrup, whole milk, and vanilla extract in a mixing bowl preferably with a spout so it easy to pour the ice cream mixture. Whisk to combine.
3. Whisk until the maple syrup is dissolved, about 2 minutes.
4. Add the heavy cream and vanilla. Whisk until the mixture is completely incorporated.
5. Cover with a plastic wrap and let the mixture cool in the refrigerator for at least 2 to 12 hours.
6. Pull out the ice cream mixture from the refrigerator and stir a few times.
7. Install the frozen ice cream maker bowl and pour the mixture into the ice cream maker.
8. Connect the machine and press ice cream and the start button.
9. About 5 minutes before then end of the churning process, add the chopped walnuts little by little into the ice cream and let it spread evenly.
10. When the cycle is finished, transfer the ice cream to an airtight freezer-safe container or serve right away. The ice cream will be soft and creamy. If you like a harder texture, allow the ice cream to freeze for 2 hours or more before serving.

Without an ice cream maker

1. Add the maple syrup, whole milk, and vanilla extract in a mixing bowl preferably with a spout so it easy to pour the ice cream mixture. Whisk to combine.
2. Whisk until the maple syrup is dissolved, about 2 minutes.
3. Add the heavy cream and vanilla. Whisk until the mixture is completely incorporated.
4. Pour the mixture in a Pyrex or stainless steel 9x13-inch pan and place it in the freezer for 30 minutes. The edges should start freezing. Using an electric handheld mixer, beat the ice cream for 1 minute.
5. Return to the freezer for another 30 minutes and beat again as before. Do this same step 4-5 times until the ice cream is harder. If at any point, the ice cream is too hard to beat, place it in the refrigerator until it becomes soft enough to beat.

6. In the last churning add the walnuts before beating and beat the ice cream one last time and the walnuts will spread.
7. Serve right away or transfer the ice cream to an airtight freezer-safe container.

Nutrition per Serving
Calories 537, fat 42 g, carbs 36 g, sugar 29 g
Protein 7 g, sodium 69 mg

Old Fashioned Coffee Ice Cream

Makes about 4 cups (½ cup per serving)

Ingredients

1 ½ cups whole milk
¾ cup sugar
1 ½ cups whole coffee beans
1 ½ cups heavy cream (separate containers)
5 large egg yolks
½ teaspoon vanilla extract
¼ teaspoon instant espresso powder

Directions

<u>*With an ice cream maker*</u>

1. Freeze the ice cream maker bowl according to manufacturer instructions, usually 12 to 24 hours.
2. Meanwhile, in a large saucepan, add the whole milk, sugar, whole coffee beans, and ½ cup of the heavy cream over medium heat. Bring the mixture to a soft simmer for about 10 to 12 minutes. Set aside.
3. Whisk until sugar is completely dissolved. Set aside.
4. In another saucepan, add the remaining 1 cup of heavy cream over medium heat. Bring the mixture to a soft simmer for about 10 to 12 minutes. Set aside.
5. In a medium bowl, pour in the egg yolks and whisk. While stirring constantly, pour in the heated 1 cup of heavy cream slowly to temper the egg yolks.
6. Heat the egg yolks and cream mixture back into the separate saucepan while whisking constantly until the mixture starts to thicken.
7. Combine the two mixtures into one clean bowl. Whisk the mixture until well incorporated.Pour the mixture into a bowl, preferably with a spot, over a fine-mesh sieve to strain all the coffee beans and coffee bean sediments.
8. Add the vanilla extract and espresso powder into the mixture. Whisk again until the mixture is well combined. Let the whole mixture cool at room temperature.
9. Cover the mixture with plastic wrap and let the mixture cool in the refrigerator for at least 2 to 12 hours.
10. Pull out the ice cream mixture from the refrigerator and stir a few times.
11. Install the frozen ice cream maker bowl and pour the mixture into the ice cream maker.
12. Connect the machine and press ice cream and the start button.
13. When the cycle is finished, transfer the ice cream to an airtight freezer-safe container or serve right away. The ice cream will be soft and creamy. If you like a harder texture, allow the ice cream to freeze for 2 hours or more before serving.

Without an ice cream maker

1. In a large saucepan, add the whole milk, sugar, whole coffee beans, and ½ cup of the heavy cream over medium heat. Bring the mixture to a soft simmer for about 10 to 12 minutes. Set aside.
2. Whisk until sugar is completely dissolved. Set aside.
3. In another saucepan, add the remaining 1 cup of heavy cream over medium heat. Bring the mixture to a soft simmer for about 10 to 12 minutes. Set aside.
4. In a medium bowl, pour in the egg yolks and whisk. While stirring constantly, pour in the heated 1 cup of heavy cream slowly to temper the egg yolks.
5. Heat the egg yolks and cream mixture back into the separate saucepan while whisking constantly until the mixture starts to thicken.
6. Combine the two mixtures into one clean bowl. Whisk the mixture until well incorporated.
7. Pour the mixture into a bowl, preferably with a spot, over a fine-mesh sieve to strain all the coffee beans and coffee bean sediments.
8. Add the vanilla extract and espresso powder into the mixture. Whisk again until the mixture is well combined. Let the whole mixture cool at room temperature.
9. Pour the mixture in a Pyrex or stainless steel 9x13-inch pan. And place in the freezer for 30 minutes. The edges should start freezing. Using an electric handheld mixer, beat the ice cream for 1 minute.
10. Return to the freezer for another 30 minutes and beat again as before. Do this same step 4-5 times until the ice cream has hardened. If at any point, the ice cream is too hard to beat, place it in the refrigerator until it becomes soft enough to beat.
11. Serve right away or transfer the ice cream to an airtight freezer-safe container.

Nutrition per Serving

Calories 420, fat 25 g, carbs 44 g, sugar 43 g
Protein 7 g, sodium 64 mg

Chocolate Covered Almond Ice Cream

Makes about 4 cups (½ cup per serving)

Ingredients

1 ¾ cup whole milk
2 cups heavy cream (separate containers)
¾ cup granulated sugar
4 egg yolks
1 ½ teaspoon vanilla extract
½ teaspoon almond extract
1 cup chocolate coated almonds

Directions

With an ice cream maker

1. Freeze the ice cream maker bowl according to manufacturer instructions, usually 12 to 24 hours.
2. Meanwhile in a large saucepan, add the whole milk, sugar, 1 cup of the heavy cream over medium heat. Bring the mixture to a soft simmer for about 10 to 12 minutes.
3. Whisk until sugar is dissolved. Remove from the heat and set aside.
4. Heat the remaining 1 cup of heavy cream in another saucepan over medium heat. Bring the mixture to a soft simmer for about 10 to 12 minutes. Set aside.
5. Pour the egg yolks in a medium bowl, and whisk. While stirring constantly, pour the heated 1 cup of heavy cream slowly to temper the egg yolks.
6. Heat the egg yolks and cream mixture back into a separate saucepan over medium-low heat while whisking constantly until the mixture starts to thicken.
7. Pour in the milk/sugar/cream mixture into the egg yolks/cream mixture. Combine the two mixtures together. Whisk the mixture until well incorporated.
8. Stir in the vanilla extract and almond extract. Mix until everything is combined.
9. Pour the whole mixture into a bowl and let it cool at room temperature.
10. Cover the mixture with plastic wrap and let the mixture cool in the refrigerator for at least 2 to 12 hours.
11. Pull out the ice cream mixture from the refrigerator and stir a few times.
12. Install the frozen ice cream maker bowl and pour the mixture into it.
13. Connect the machine and press ice cream and the start button.
14. About 5 minutes before then end of the churning process, add the chocolate-coated almonds little by little into the ice cream and let it spread evenly.
15. When the cycle is finished, transfer the ice cream to an airtight freezer-safe container or serve right away. The ice cream will be soft and creamy. If you like a harder texture, allow the ice cream to freeze for 2 hours or more before serving.

Without an ice cream maker

1. In a large saucepan, add the whole milk, sugar, 1 cup of the heavy cream over medium heat. Bring the mixture to a soft simmer for about 10 to 12 minutes.
2. Whisk until sugar is dissolved. Remove from the heat and set aside.
3. Heat the remaining 1 cup of heavy cream in another saucepan over medium heat. Bring the mixture to a soft simmer for about 10 to 12 minutes. Set aside.
4. Pour the egg yolks in a medium bowl, and whisk. While stirring constantly, pour the heated 1 cup of heavy cream slowly to temper the egg yolks.
5. Heat the egg yolks and cream mixture back into a separate saucepan over medium-low heat while whisking constantly until the mixture starts to thicken.
6. Pour in the milk/sugar/cream mixture into the egg yolks/cream mixture. Combine the two mixtures together. Whisk the mixture until well incorporated.
7. Stir in the vanilla extract and almond extract. Mix until everything is combined.
8. Pour the mixture in a Pyrex or stainless steel 9x13-inch pan. And place in the freezer for 30 minutes. The edges should start freezing. Using an electric handheld mixer, beat the ice cream for 1 minute.
9. Return to the freezer for another 30 minutes and beat again as before. Do this same step 4-5 times until the ice cream has hardened. If at any point, the ice cream is too hard to beat, place it in the refrigerator until it becomes soft enough to beat.
10. In the last churning add the chocolate-coated almonds before beating and beat the ice cream one last time, so the almonds will spread.
11. Serve right away or transfer the ice cream to an airtight freezer-safe container.

Nutrition per Serving

Calories 537, fat 36 g, carbs 47 g, sugar 44 g, protein 10 g, sodium 74 mg

Banana Ice Cream

Makes about 4 cups (½ cup per serving)

Ingredients

1 cup whole milk
2 cups chilled heavy cream
2/3 cup granulated sugar
5 egg yolks
3 large bananas
1 teaspoon vanilla extract
1 tablespoon rum extract
1 cup chocolate chips
Chocolate shavings for garnish

Directions

With an ice cream maker

1. Freeze the ice cream maker bowl according to manufacturer instructions, usually 12 to 24 hours.
2. Meanwhile in a large saucepan, add the whole milk and granulated sugar. over medium heat. Bring the mixture to a soft simmer for about 10 to 12 minutes. Set aside.
3. You will know when it's ready, the edges of the pan will start to form small bubbles. Whisk until sugar is all dissolved in the milk. Remove from the heat.
4. Pour in the egg yolks in a medium bowl and whisk. While stirring constantly, pour in the hot milk mixture slowly to temper the egg yolks.
5. Heat the whole mixture over medium heat again until the mixture starts to thicken. Set aside.
6. In a large bowl, add the chilled heavy cream. Hold a fine-mesh sieve over it and pour the hot egg yolks/milk mixture to strain and remove any cooked pieces of the egg yolks.
7. Pour the vanilla extract and rum extract into the mixture. Whisk to combine or until the whole mixture is completely incorporated.
8. Take half of the mixture and pour it in a high-speed blender alongside with the bananas.
9. Blitz until you get a creamy, evenly mixture. Pour it back to the remaining cream. Mix to combine. Let cool at room temperature.
10. Cover the mixture with plastic wrap and let the mixture cool in the refrigerator for at least 2 to 12 hours.
11. Pull out the ice cream mixture from the refrigerator and stir a few times.
12. Install the frozen ice cream maker bowl and pour the mixture into the ice cream maker.
13. Connect the machine and press ice cream and the start button.

14. About 5 minutes before then end of the churning process, add the chocolate chips little by little into the ice cream and let them mix in.
15. When the cycle is finished, transfer the ice cream to an airtight freezer-safe container or serve right away. The ice cream will be soft and creamy. If you like a harder texture, allow the ice cream to freeze for 2 hours or more before serving.
16. Serve with chocolate shavings on top.

Without an ice cream maker

1. In a large saucepan, add the whole milk and granulated sugar. over medium heat. Bring the mixture to a soft simmer for about 10 to 12 minutes. Set aside.
2. You will know when it's ready, the edges of the pan will start to form small bubbles. Whisk until sugar is all dissolved in the milk. Remove from the heat.
3. Pour in the egg yolks in a medium bowl and whisk. While stirring constantly, pour in the hot milk mixture slowly to temper the egg yolks.
4. Heat the whole mixture over medium heat again until the mixture starts to thicken. Set aside.
5. In a large bowl, add the chilled heavy cream. Hold a fine-mesh sieve over it and pour the hot egg yolks/milk mixture to strain and remove any cooked pieces of the egg yolks.
6. Pour the vanilla extract and rum extract into the mixture. Whisk to combine or until the whole mixture is completely incorporated.
7. Take half of the mixture and pour it in a high-speed blender alongside with the bananas.
8. Blitz until you get a creamy, evenly mixture. Pour it back to the remaining cream. Mix to combine. Let cool at room temperature.
9. Pour the mixture in a Pyrex or stainless steel 9x13-inch pan. And place in the freezer for 30 minutes. The edges should start freezing. Using an electric handheld mixer, beat the ice cream for 1 minute.
10. Return to the freezer for another 30 minutes and beat again as before. Do this same step 4-5 times until the ice cream has hardened. If at any point, the ice cream is too hard to beat, place it in the refrigerator until it becomes soft enough to beat.
11. In the last churning add the chocolate chips before beating and beat the ice cream one last time, so the chocolate chips will spread.
12. Serve right away or transfer the ice cream to an airtight freezer-safe container.
13. Serve with chocolate shavings on top.

Nutrition per Serving

Calories 955, fat 60 g, carbs 85 g, sugar 71 g
Protein 10 g, sodium 69 mg

Reese's Peanut Butter Cups Ice Cream

Makes about 4 cups (½ cup per serving)

Ingredients

1 cup whole milk

2 cups chilled heavy cream

¼ cup dark chocolate syrup

10 Reese's Peanut Butter cups, cut into small pieces

1 tsp vanilla extract

Directions

With an ice cream maker

1. Freeze the ice cream maker bowl according to manufacturer instructions, usually 12 to 24 hours.
2. In a high-speed blender, add the cream, milk, and chocolate syrup.
3. Blitz until you get a smooth and creamy mixture.
4. Pour the mixture in a clean bowl, preferably with a spout, and stir in the vanilla extract. Whisk to combine.
5. Cover the mixture with plastic wrap and let the mixture cool in the refrigerator for at least 2 to 12 hours.
6. Pull out the ice cream mixture from the refrigerator and stir a few times.
7. Install the frozen ice cream maker bowl and pour the mixture into the ice cream maker.
8. Connect the machine and press ice cream and the start button.
9. About 5 minutes before then end of the churning process, add the cut up Reese's peanut butter cups little by little into the ice cream and let it spread evenly.
10. When the cycle is finished, transfer the ice cream to an airtight freezer-safe container or serve right away. The ice cream will be soft and creamy. If you like a harder texture, allow the ice cream to freeze for 2 hours or more before serving.

Without an ice cream maker

1. In a high-speed blender, add the cream, milk, and chocolate syrup.
2. Blitz until you get a smooth and creamy mixture.
3. Pour the mixture in a Pyrex or stainless steel 9x13-inch pan and stir in the vanilla extract. Whisk to combine.
4. Place in the freezer for 30 minutes. The edges should start freezing. Using an electric handheld mixer, beat the ice cream for 1 minute.
5. Return to the freezer for another 30 minutes and beat again as before. Do this same step 4-5 times until the ice cream has hardened. If at any point, the ice cream is too hard to beat, place it in the refrigerator until it becomes soft enough to beat.
6. In the last churning add the cut-up Reese's peanut butter cups before beating and beat the ice cream one last time, so the Reese's will spread.

7. Serve right away or transfer the ice cream to an airtight freezer-safe container.

Nutrition per Serving
Calories 460, fat 30 g, carbs 44 g, sugar 41 g
Protein 8 g, sodium 58 mg

Birthday Cake Ice Cream

Makes about 4 cups (½ cup per serving)

Ingredients
1 ½ cup whole milk
1 ½ cups heavy cream
1 cup granulated sugar
2 teaspoons vanilla extract
½ cup Rainbow Sprinkles
2 vanilla muffins

Directions
With an ice cream maker

1. Freeze the ice cream maker bowl according to manufacturer instructions, usually 12 to 24 hours.
2. Meanwhile in a large saucepan, add the whole milk, heavy cream, and sugar over medium heat. Bring the mixture to a soft simmer for about 10 to 12 minutes. Set aside.
3. Whisk constantly until the sugar is dissolved. When the sugar is dissolved completely, pour the mixture into a clean bowl, preferably with a spout.
4. Stir in the vanilla extract and let cool at room temperature completely.
5. Cover the mixture with plastic wrap and let the mixture cool in the refrigerator for at least 2 to 12 hours.
6. Prepare to chop up the muffins into small pieces, so you can later add them to the ice cream mixture.
7. Pull out the ice cream mixture from the refrigerator and stir a few times.
8. Install the frozen ice cream maker bowl and pour the mixture into the ice cream maker.
9. Connect the machine and press ice cream and the start button.
10. About 5 minutes before then end of the churning process, add the rainbow sprinkles and chopped muffins little by little into the ice cream and let it mix in.
11. When the cycle is finished, transfer the ice cream to an airtight freezer-safe container or serve right away. The ice cream will be soft and creamy. If you like a harder texture, allow the ice cream to freeze for 2 hours or more before serving.

Without an ice cream maker

1. In a large saucepan, add the whole milk, heavy cream, and sugar over medium heat. Bring the mixture to a soft simmer for about 10 to 12 minutes. Set aside.
2. Whisk constantly until the sugar is dissolved. When the sugar is dissolved completely, pour the mixture into a clean bowl, preferably with a spout.
3. Stir in the vanilla extract and let cool at room temperature completely.

4. Prepare to chop up the muffins into small pieces, so you can later add them to the ice cream mixture.
5. Pour the mixture in a Pyrex or stainless steel 9x13-inch pan. And place in the freezer for 30 minutes. The edges should start freezing. Using an electric handheld mixer, beat the ice cream for 1 minute.
6. Return to the freezer for another 30 minutes and beat again as before. Do this same step 4-5 times until the ice cream has hardened. If at any point, the ice cream is too hard to beat, place it in the refrigerator until it becomes soft enough to beat.
7. In the last churning add the sprinkles and diced muffins before beating and beat the ice cream one last time, so the sprinkles and the muffins will spread.
8. Serve right away or transfer the ice cream to an airtight freezer-safe container.

Nutrition per Serving
Calories 475, fat 22 g, carbs 68 g, sugar 62 g
Protein 5 g, sodium 99 mg

Cotton Candy Ice Cream

Makes about 3 cups (½ cup per serving)

Ingredients

1 cups whole milk
2 cup heavy whipping cream
¾ cup granulated sugar
1 teaspoons vanilla extract
½ cup cotton candy syrup
Food coloring (optional)

Directions

With an ice cream maker

1. Freeze the ice cream maker bowl according to manufacturer instructions, usually 12 to 24 hours.
2. Meanwhile in a large mixing bowl, add the milk and sugar. Whisk until sugar is dissolved completely.
3. Pour in the vanilla, cream, and cotton candy syrup. Whisk again to combine.
4. Add food coloring according to the desired color.
5. Cover the mixture with plastic wrap and let the mixture cool in the refrigerator for at least 2 to 12 hours.
6. Pull out the ice cream mixture from the refrigerator and whisk in the heavy cream. Mix it well.
7. Install the frozen ice cream maker bowl and pour the mixture into the ice cream maker.
8. Connect the machine and press ice cream and the start button.
9. When the cycle is finished, transfer the ice cream to an airtight freezer-safe container or serve right away. The ice cream will be soft and creamy. If you like a harder texture, allow the ice cream to freeze for 2 hours or more before serving.

Without an ice cream maker

1. In a large mixing bowl, add the milk and sugar. Whisk until sugar is dissolved completely.
2. Pour in the vanilla, cream, and cotton candy syrup. Whisk again to combine.
3. Add food coloring according to the desired color.
4. Pour the mixture in a Pyrex or stainless steel 9x13-inch pan. And place in the freezer for 30 minutes. The edges should start freezing. Using an electric handheld mixer, beat the ice cream for 1 minute.
5. Return to the freezer for another 30 minutes and beat again as before. Do this same step 4-5 times until the ice cream has hardened. If at any point, the ice cream is too hard to beat, place it in the refrigerator until it becomes soft enough to beat.

6. Serve right away or transfer the ice cream to an airtight freezer-safe container to serve it later.

Nutrition per Serving
Calories 644, fat 37 g, carbs 66 g, sugar 58 g
Protein 16 g, sodium 141 mg

Stracciatella Ice Cream

Makes about 4 cups (½ cup per serving)

Ingredients
2 cups whole milk
1 cup heavy cream
⅔ cup granulated sugar
1 tablespoon honey
2 teaspoons vanilla extract
4 egg yolks
2 tablespoons butter
4 oz. dark chocolate, finely chopped

Directions
With an ice cream maker

1. Freeze the ice cream maker bowl according to manufacturer instructions, usually 12 to 24 hours.
2. In a large saucepan, add the whole milk, heavy cream, granulated sugar, and honey over medium heat. Bring the mixture to a soft simmer for about 10 to 12 minutes. Set aside.
3. Whisk constantly until the sugar and honey are dissolved.
4. When the sugar dissolves slowly pour the hot milk and cream mixture to a bowl with the egg yolks while whisking constantly.
5. Pour the mixture back into the saucepan and heat the whole egg yolk and milk mixture over medium heat for 3-4 minutes until it's creamy and strain the whole mixture in a clean bowl, preferably with a spout, over a fine-mesh sieve.
6. Cover the mixture with plastic wrap and let the mixture cool in the refrigerator for at least 2 to 12 hours.
7. Pull out the ice cream mixture from the refrigerator and stir a few times.
8. Install the frozen ice cream maker bowl and pour the mixture into the ice cream maker.
9. Connect the machine and press ice cream and the start button.
10. About 5 to 6 minutes before then end of the churning process, melt the chocolate and butter in a microwave-safe bowl for 2 minutes, stirring every 30-40 seconds.
11. Transfer the melted chocolate mixture little by little into the ice cream and let it mix in.
12. When the cycle is finished, transfer the ice cream to an airtight freezer-safe container or serve right away. The ice cream will be soft and creamy. If you like a harder texture, allow the ice cream to freeze for 2 hours or more before serving.

Without an ice cream maker

1. In a large saucepan, add the whole milk, heavy cream, granulated sugar, and honey over medium heat. Bring the mixture to a soft simmer for about 10 to 12 minutes. Set aside.
2. Whisk constantly until the sugar and honey are dissolved.
3. When the sugar dissolves slowly pour the hot milk and cream mixture to a bowl with the egg yolks while whisking constantly.
4. Pour the mixture back into the saucepan and heat the whole egg yolk and milk mixture over medium heat for 3-4 minutes until it's creamy and strain the whole mixture in a clean bowl, preferably with a spout, over a fine-mesh sieve.
5. Pour the mixture in a Pyrex or stainless steel 9x13-inch pan. And place in the freezer for 30 minutes. The edges should start freezing. Using an electric handheld mixer, beat the ice cream for 1 minute.
6. Return to the freezer for another 30 minutes and beat again as before. Do this same step 4-5 times until the ice cream has hardened. If at any point, the ice cream is too hard to beat, place it in the refrigerator until it becomes soft enough to beat.
7. In the last churning add the melted chocolate and butter together sealed in the piping bag so you can drizzle it all over the mixture before beating and beat the ice cream one last time, so the chocolate will break and spread. Serve right away or transfer the ice cream to an airtight freezer-safe container to serve it later.

Nutrition per Serving

Calories 580, fat 34 g, carbs 62 g, sugar 59 g, protein 10 g, sodium 132 mg

Coconut Ice Cream

Makes about 4 cups (½ cup per serving)

Ingredients

1 ½ cups canned coconut milk
½ cup heavy cream
½ cup granulated sugar
2 teaspoons vanilla extract
½ cup coconut flakes

Directions

With an ice cream maker

1. Freeze the ice cream maker bowl according to manufacturer instructions, usually 12 to 24 hours.
2. Meanwhile in a large bowl, add the coconut milk, heavy cream, and granulated sugar. Whisk to combine.
3. Stir for about 5 minutes until the sugar is dissolved and stir in the vanilla extract.
4. Cover the mixture with plastic wrap and let the mixture cool in the refrigerator for at least 2 to 12 hours.
5. Pull out the ice cream mixture from the refrigerator and stir a few times.
6. Install the frozen ice cream maker bowl and pour the mixture into it.
7. Connect the machine and press ice cream and the start button.
8. About 5 to 6 minutes before then end of the churning process, add in the coconut flakes little by little into the ice cream and let it mix in.
9. When the cycle is finished, transfer the ice cream to an airtight freezer-safe container or serve right away. If you like a harder texture, allow the ice cream to freeze for 2 hours or more before serving.

Without an ice cream maker

1. In a large bowl, add the coconut milk, heavy cream, and granulated sugar. Whisk to combine.
2. Stir for about 5 minutes until the sugar is dissolved and stir in the vanilla extract.
3. Pour the mixture in a Pyrex or stainless steel 9x13-inch pan. And place in the freezer for 30 minutes. The edges should start freezing. Using an electric handheld mixer, beat the ice cream for 1 minute.
4. Return to the freezer for another 30 minutes and beat again as before. Do this same step 4-5 times until the ice cream has hardened. If at any point, the ice cream is too hard to beat, place it in the refrigerator until it becomes soft enough to beat.
5. In the last churning, add the coconut flakes to the mixture and beat the ice cream one last time, so the coconut flakes will spread evenly.
6. Serve right away or transfer the ice cream to an airtight freezer-safe container to serve it later.

Nutrition per Serving

Calories 394, fat 30g, carbs 32 g, sugar 29 g
Protein 3 g, sodium 21 mg

Orange Ice Cream

Makes about 4 cups (½ cup per serving)

Ingredients

½ cup whole milk
1 ½ cup heavy cream
2 cups freshly squeezed orange juice
½ cup granulated sugar
1 tablespoon freshly grated orange zest
2 teaspoons vanilla extract

Directions

With an ice cream maker

1. Freeze the ice cream maker bowl according to manufacturer instructions, usually 12 to 24 hours.
2. Meanwhile in a large bowl, add the whole milk, heavy cream, orange juice, orange zest, and granulated sugar. Whisk to combine.
3. Stir for about 5 minutes until the sugar is dissolved and stir in the vanilla extract.
4. Cover the mixture with plastic wrap and let the mixture cool in the refrigerator for at least 2 to 12 hours.
5. Pull out the ice cream mixture from the refrigerator and stir a few times.
6. Install the frozen ice cream maker bowl and pour the mixture into it.
7. Connect the machine and press ice cream and the start button.
8. When the cycle is finished, transfer the ice cream to an airtight freezer-safe container or serve right away. If you like a harder texture, allow the ice cream to freeze for 2 hours or more before serving.

Without an ice cream maker

1. In a large bowl, add the whole milk, heavy cream, orange juice, orange zest, and granulated sugar. Whisk to combine.
2. Stir for about 5 minutes until the sugar is dissolved and stir in the vanilla extract.
3. Pour the mixture in a Pyrex or stainless steel 9x13-inch pan. And place in the freezer for 30 minutes. The edges should start freezing. Using an electric handheld mixer, beat the ice cream for 1 minute.
4. Return to the freezer for another 30 minutes and beat again as before. Do this same step 4-5 times until the ice cream has hardened. If at any point, the ice cream is too hard to beat, place it in the refrigerator until it becomes soft enough to beat.
5. Serve right away or transfer the ice cream to an airtight freezer-safe container to serve it later.

Nutrition per Serving

Calories 331, fat 18 g, carbs 41 g, sugar 37 g
Protein 3 g, sodium 31 mg

Passion Fruit Ice Cream

Makes about 4 cups (½ cup per serving)

Ingredients
1 can sweetened condensed milk
2 cups heavy cream
2 cups, 14 oz. can of passion fruit pulp
1 teaspoon vanilla extract
1/3 cup fresh passion fruit pulp
2/3 cup granulated sugar
1 teaspoon cornstarch
1 tablespoon water

Directions
With an ice cream maker

1. Freeze the ice cream maker bowl according to manufacturer instructions, usually 12 to 24 hours.
2. Meanwhile in a large bowl add the condensed milk, heavy cream, and passion fruit pulp. Whisk to combine.
3. Stir until everything is combined and stir in the vanilla extract.
4. Cover the mixture with plastic wrap and let the mixture cool in the refrigerator for at least 2 to 12 hours.
5. Meanwhile, in a medium-sized saucepan, heat the fresh passion fruit pulp with the sugar over medium heat. Bring the mixture to a soft simmer for about 10 to 12 minutes. Set aside.
6. In a small glass, mix the cornstarch with the water, this process is known as a slurry.
7. Mix the slurry in the saucepan with the passion fruit mixture. Whisk to combine.
8. Pour the mixture in a bowl and set aside. Let the whole passion fruit sauce cool completely.
9. Pull out the ice cream mixture from the refrigerator and stir a few times.
10. Install the frozen ice cream maker bowl and pour the mixture into the ice cream maker.
11. Connect the machine and press ice cream and the start button.
12. About 5 to 6 minutes before then end of the churning process, add in the passion fruit sauce little by little into the ice cream and let it mix in.
13. When the cycle is finished, transfer the ice cream to an airtight freezer-safe container or serve right away. If you like a harder texture, allow the ice cream to freeze for 2 hours or more before serving.

Without an ice cream maker

1. In a large bowl add the condensed milk, heavy cream, and passion fruit pulp. Whisk to combine.
2. Stir until everything is combined and stir in the vanilla extract.
3. Meanwhile, in a medium-sized saucepan, heat the fresh passion fruit pulp with the sugar over medium heat. Bring the mixture to a soft simmer for about 10 to 12 minutes. Set aside.
4. In a small glass, mix the cornstarch with the water. This process is known as a slurry.
5. Mix the slurry in the saucepan with the passion fruit mixture. Whisk to combine.
6. Pour the mixture in a bowl and set aside. Let the whole passion fruit sauce cool completely.
7. Pour the mixture in a Pyrex or stainless steel 9x13-inch pan. And place in the freezer for 30 minutes. The edges should start freezing. Using an electric handheld mixer, beat the ice cream for 1 minute.
8. Return to the freezer for another 30 minutes and beat again as before. Do this same step 4-5 times until the ice cream has hardened. If at any point, the ice cream is too hard to beat, place it in the refrigerator until it becomes soft enough to beat.
9. In the last churning add the passion fruit sauce and beat the ice cream one last time, so the sauce will be evenly spread.
10. Serve right away or transfer the ice cream to an airtight freezer-safe container to serve it later.

Nutrition per Serving

Calories 610, fat 29 g, carbs 83 g, sugar 78 g, protein 9 g, sodium 128 mg

Amaretti Ice Cream

Makes about 4 cups (½ cup per serving)

Ingredients

1 ½ cup whole milk
1 cup heavy cream
½ cup granulated sugar
1 teaspoon vanilla extract
1/3 cup amaretto liqueur
2 egg whites
4 oz. amaretti cookies

Directions

With an ice cream maker

1. Freeze the ice cream maker bowl according to manufacturer instructions, usually 12 to 24 hours.
2. Meanwhile in a large saucepan, add the whole milk, heavy cream, and sugar over medium heat. Bring the mixture to a soft simmer for about 10 to 12 minutes.
3. Whisk constantly until the sugar is dissolved.
4. When the sugar is completely dissolved, pour the mixture in a clean bowl, preferably with a spout, and set aside. Stir in the vanilla extract and amaretto liqueur. Let the whole mixture to cool completely.
5. Cover the mixture with plastic wrap and let the mixture cool in the refrigerator for at least 2 to 12 hours.
6. Meanwhile, beat the egg whites with the help of a hand mixer until stiff peaks form.
7. After chilling the ice cream base, fold in the beaten egg whites into the ice cream base.
8. Pull out the ice cream mixture from the refrigerator and stir a few times.
9. Install the frozen ice cream maker bowl and pour the mixture into the ice cream maker.
10. Connect the machine and press ice cream and the start button.
11. About 5 minutes before the end of the churning process, add the crushed amaretti into small pieces little by little into the ice cream and let it mix in.
12. When the cycle is finished, transfer the ice cream to an airtight freezer-safe container or serve right away. The ice cream will be soft and creamy. If you like a harder texture, allow the ice cream to freeze for 2 hours or more before serving.

Without an ice cream maker

1. In a large saucepan, add the whole milk, heavy cream, and sugar over medium heat. Bring the mixture to a soft simmer for about 10 to 12 minutes.
2. Whisk constantly until the sugar is dissolved.

3. When the sugar is completely dissolved, pour the mixture in a clean bowl, preferably with a spout, and set aside. Stir in the vanilla extract and amaretto liqueur. Let the whole mixture to cool completely.
4. Meanwhile, beat the egg whites with the help of a hand mixer until stiff peaks form.
5. After chilling the ice cream base, fold in the beaten egg whites into the ice cream base.
6. Pour the mixture in a Pyrex or stainless steel 9x13-inch pan. And place in the freezer for 30 minutes. The edges should start freezing. Using an electric handheld mixer, beat the ice cream for 1 minute.
7. Return to the freezer for another 30 minutes and beat again as before. Do this same step 4-5 times until the ice cream has hardened. If at any point, the ice cream is too hard to beat, place it in the refrigerator until it becomes soft enough to beat.
8. In the last churning, add the crushed amaretti and beat the ice cream one last time, so the amaretti will spread.
9. Serve right away or transfer the ice cream to an airtight freezer-safe container.

Nutrition per Serving

Calories 443, fat 16 g, carbs 55 g, sugar 67 g
Protein 9 g, sodium 104 mg

Vanilla Cherry Ice Cream

Makes about 4 cups (½ cup per serving)

Ingredients

1 cup milk
2 cup chilled heavy cream
¾ cup white sugar
2 ½ cups cherries, pitted and halved
1 teaspoon vanilla extract
1 teaspoon almond extract

Directions

With an ice cream maker

1. Freeze the ice cream maker bowl according to manufacturer instructions, usually 12 to 24 hours.
2. Meanwhile in a mixing bowl combine the condensed milk, almond extract, and vanilla extract. Whisk to combine.
3. In another mixing bowl, whip up the heavy cream into stiff peaks. Pour the condensed milk mixture. Fold gently.
4. In a high-speed blender or food processor, blitz 1 ½ cups of the cherries until smooth and pureed.
5. Pour the pureed cherries into the condensed milk and whipped cream mixture and fold it gently.
6. Cover the mixture with plastic wrap and let the mixture cool in the refrigerator for at least 2 to 12 hours.
7. Pull out the ice cream mixture from the refrigerator and whisk in the heavy cream to mix it well.
8. Install the frozen ice cream maker bowl and pour the mixture into it.
9. Connect the machine and press ice cream and the start button.
10. About 5 to 6 minutes before then end of the churning process, remaining 1 cup of pitted cherries, roughly chopped little by little into the ice cream and let it mix in.
11. When the cycle is finished, transfer the ice cream to an airtight freezer-safe container or serve right away. The ice cream will be soft and creamy. If you like a harder texture, allow the ice cream to freeze for 2 hours or more before serving.

Without an ice cream maker

1. In a mixing bowl combine the condensed milk, almond extract, and vanilla extract. Whisk to combine.
2. In another mixing bowl, whip up the heavy cream into stiff peaks. Pour the condensed milk mixture. Fold gently.
3. In a high-speed blender or food processor, blitz 1 ½ cups of the cherries until smooth and pureed.

4. Pour the pureed cherries into the condensed milk and whipped cream mixture and fold it gently.
5. Let cool at room temperature.
6. Pour the mixture in a Pyrex or stainless steel 9x13-inch pan. And place in the freezer for 30 minutes. The edges should start freezing. Using an electric handheld mixer, beat the ice cream for 1 minute.
7. Return to the freezer for another 30 minutes and beat again as before. Do this same step 4-5 times until the ice cream has hardened. If at any point, the ice cream is too hard to beat, place it in the refrigerator until it becomes soft enough to beat.
8. In the last churning add the remaining 1 cup of pitted cherries that are roughly chopped and beat the ice cream one last time, so the cherries will spread evenly.
9. Serve right away or transfer the ice cream to an airtight freezer-safe container to serve it later.

Nutrition per Serving

Calories 363, fat 23 g, carbs 29 g, sugar 29 g, protein 3 g, sodium 67 mg

Coconut Almond Chocolate Chip Ice Cream

Makes about 4 cups (½ cup per serving)

Ingredients

1 can (14-ounce) sweetened condensed milk
2 cups heavy cream
1 teaspoon vanilla extract
½ teaspoon coconut extract
½ cup coconut flakes
½ cup white chocolate chips

Directions

With an ice cream maker

1. Freeze the ice cream maker bowl according to manufacturer instructions, usually 12 to 24 hours.
2. Meanwhile in a large bowl, add the condensed milk, heavy cream, vanilla extract, and coconut extract.
3. Mix until everything is combined.
4. Cover the mixture with plastic wrap and let cool in the refrigerator for at least 2 to 12 hours.
5. In another mixing bowl, add the coconut flakes, chocolate chips, and almond slices. Stir to combine.
6. Pull out the ice cream mixture from the refrigerator and stir a few times.
7. Install the frozen ice cream maker bowl and pour the mixture into it.
8. Connect the machine and press ice cream and the start button.
9. About 5 to 6 minutes before then end of the churning process, add the mixture of coconut flakes, chocolate chips, and almond slices little by little into the ice cream and let it mix in.
10. When the cycle is finished, transfer the ice cream to an airtight freezer-safe container or serve right away. The ice cream will be soft and creamy. If you like a harder texture, allow the ice cream to freeze for 2 hours or more before serving.

Without an ice cream maker

1. In a large bowl, add the condensed milk, heavy cream, vanilla extract, and coconut extract.
2. Mix until everything is combined.
3. In another mixing bowl, add the coconut flakes, chocolate chips, and almond slices. Stir to combine.
4. Pour the mixture in a Pyrex or stainless steel 9x13-inch pan. And place in the freezer for 30 minutes. The edges should start freezing. Using an electric handheld mixer, beat the ice cream for 1 minute.

5. Return to the freezer for another 30 minutes and beat again as before. Do this same step 4-5 times until the ice cream has hardened. If at any point, the ice cream is too hard to beat, place it in the refrigerator until it becomes soft enough to beat.
6. In the last churning add the mixture of coconut, chocolate, and almonds and beat the ice cream one last time, so the coconut, chocolate, and almonds will spread evenly.
7. Serve right away or transfer the ice cream to an airtight freezer-safe container.

Nutrition per Serving
Calories 827, fat 48 g, carbs 87 g, sugar 80 g
Protein 17 g, sodium 202 mg

Dark Chocolate Ice Cream

Makes about 4 cups (½ cup per serving)

Ingredients

1 ½ cups whole milk
2 cups heavy cream
6 tablespoons good quality cocoa powder
8 oz. dark chocolate with a minimum 70% cocoa solids
6 egg yolks
½ cup granulated sugar
1 teaspoon vanilla extract
1 tablespoon dark rum

Directions

With an ice cream maker

1. Freeze the ice cream maker bowl according to manufacturer instructions, usually 12 to 24 hours.
2. Meanwhile in a saucepan, add the milk, cream, and cocoa powder over medium heat. Bring the mixture to a soft simmer for about 10 to 12 minutes. Set aside.
3. In a mixing bowl, add the egg yolks and sugar and whisk to combine. While whisking constantly, pour the hot milk, cream, and cocoa mixture into the egg yolks mixture slowly.
4. Pour in the heavy cream and whisk until the mixture is incorporated. Transfer everything in the saucepan to cook for 3-4 minutes more until it's creamy and slightly thickened.
5. Strain the hot mixture over a fine-mesh sieve in a clean bowl, preferably with a spout, with dark chocolate chopped in smaller pieces in it.
6. Let it sit for 5 minutes and stir with a spatula until everything is melted and fully combined. Stir in the vanilla extract and dark rum. Mix again to combine.
7. Cover the mixture with plastic wrap and let the mixture cool in the refrigerator for at least 2 to 12 hours.
8. Pull out the ice cream mixture from the refrigerator and stir a few times.
9. Install the frozen ice cream maker bowl and pour the mixture into the ice cream maker.
10. Connect the machine and press ice cream and the start button.
11. When the cycle is finished, transfer the ice cream to an airtight freezer-safe container or serve right away. The ice cream will be soft and creamy. If you like a harder texture, allow the ice cream to freeze for 2 hours or more before serving.

Without an ice cream maker

1. In a saucepan, add the milk, cream, and cocoa powder over medium heat. Bring the mixture to a soft simmer for about 10 to 12 minutes. Set aside.
2. In a mixing bowl, add the egg yolks and sugar and whisk to combine. While whisking constantly, pour the hot milk, cream, and cocoa mixture into the egg yolks mixture slowly.
3. Pour in the heavy cream and whisk until the mixture is incorporated. Transfer everything in the saucepan to cook for 3-4 minutes more until it's creamy and slightly thickened.
4. Strain the hot mixture over a fine-mesh sieve in a clean bowl, preferably with a spout, with dark chocolate chopped in smaller pieces in it.
5. Let it sit for 5 minutes and stir with a spatula until everything is melted and fully combined. Stir in the vanilla extract and dark rum. Mix again to combine.
6. Pour the mixture in a Pyrex or stainless steel 9x13-inch pan. And place in the freezer for 30 minutes. The edges should start freezing. Using an electric handheld mixer, beat the ice cream for 1 minute.
7. Return to the freezer for another 30 minutes and beat again as before. Do this same step 4-5 times until the ice cream has hardened. If at any point, the ice cream is too hard to beat, place it in the refrigerator until it becomes soft enough to beat.
8. Serve right away or transfer the ice cream to an airtight freezer-safe container.

Nutrition per Serving

Calories 630, fat 40 g, carbs 71 g, sugar 61 g, protein 13 g, sodium 95 mg

Rocky Road Ice Cream

Makes about 4 cups (½ cup per serving)

Ingredients

1 cup granulated sugar
½ cup cocoa powder
2 cups heavy cream
1 ½ cup milk
½ cup chocolate chips
½ cup chopped almonds
1 cup mini marshmallows

Directions

With an ice cream maker

1. Freeze the ice cream maker bowl according to manufacturer instructions, usually 12 to 24 hours.
2. Meanwhile in a large saucepan, add the granulated sugar, cocoa powder, heavy cream, and milk over medium heat. Bring the mixture to a soft simmer for about 10 to 12 minutes.
3. Stir until the cocoa powder and sugar are dissolved in the mixture and set aside.
4. Cover with a plastic wrap and let the mixture cool in the refrigerator for at least 2 to 12 hours.
5. Prepare a clean bowl, add the chocolate chips, chopped almonds, and mini marshmallows. Set aside for later use.
6. Pull out the ice cream mixture from the refrigerator and stir a few times.
7. Install the frozen ice cream maker bowl and pour the mixture into it.
8. Connect the machine and press ice cream and the start button.
9. About 5 to 6 minutes before then end of the churning process, add the chopped hazelnuts, chocolate chips, and mini marshmallows little by little into the ice cream and let them mix in.
10. When the cycle is finished, transfer the ice cream to an airtight freezer-safe container or serve right away. The ice cream will be soft and creamy. If you like a harder texture, allow the ice cream to freeze for 2 hours or more before serving.

Without an ice cream maker

1. In a large saucepan, add the granulated sugar, cocoa powder, heavy cream, and milk over medium heat. Bring the mixture to a soft simmer for about 10 to 12 minutes.
2. Stir until the cocoa powder and sugar are dissolved in the mixture and set aside.
3. Prepare a clean bowl, add the chocolate chips, chopped almonds, and mini marshmallows. Set aside for later use.

4. Pour the cocoa powder/sugar mixture in a Pyrex or stainless steel 9x13-inch pan. And place in the freezer for 30 minutes. The edges should start freezing. Using an electric handheld mixer, beat the ice cream for 1 minute.
5. Return to the freezer for another 30 minutes and beat again as before. Do this same step 4-5 times until the ice cream has hardened. If at any point, the ice cream is too hard to beat, place it in the refrigerator until it becomes soft enough to beat.
6. In the last churning add the chopped almonds, chocolate chips, and mini marshmallows mix and beat the ice cream one last time, so the add-ons will spread evenly.
7. Serve right away or transfer the ice cream to an airtight freezer-safe container.

Nutrition per Serving

Calories 691, fat 38 g, carbs 88 g, sugar 72 g
Protein 10 g, sodium 96 mg

Mint Chocolate Chip Ice Cream

Makes about 4 cups (½ cup per serving)

Ingredients

2 cups heavy cream, chilled
1 cup whole milk, chilled
1 cup sugar
½-1 teaspoon mint extract, to taste
½ cup semi-sweet chocolate chips or chopped semi-sweet chocolate
Green food coloring, a few drops (optional)

Directions

With an ice cream maker

1. Freeze the ice cream maker bowl according to manufacturer instructions, usually 12 to 24 hours.
2. Meanwhile, add the heavy cream, whole milk, sugar, and vanilla in a medium mixing bowl. Mix until well blended.
3. Stir until the sugar dissolves. Add mint extract and green food coloring, if desired. Mix well.
4. Cover with a plastic wrap and let the mixture cool in the refrigerator for at least 2 to 12 hours.
5. Pull out the ice cream mixture from the refrigerator and stir a few times.
6. Install the frozen ice cream maker bowl and pour the mixture into it.
7. Connect the machine and press ice cream and the start button.
8. About 5 to 6 minutes before then end of the churning process, add the chocolate chips little by little into the ice cream and let them mix in.
9. When the cycle is finished, transfer the ice cream to an airtight freezer-safe container or serve right away. The ice cream will be soft and creamy. If you like a harder texture, allow the ice cream to freeze for 2 hours or more before serving.

Without an ice cream maker

1. Add the heavy cream, whole milk, mint extract, sugar, and vanilla in a medium mixing bowl. Mix until well blended.
2. Stir until the sugar dissolves.
3. Pour the mixture in a Pyrex or stainless steel 9x13-inch pan. And place in the freezer for 30 minutes. The edges should start freezing. Using an electric handheld mixer, beat the ice cream for 1 minute.
4. Return to the freezer for another 30 minutes and beat again as before. Do this same step 4-5 times until the ice cream has hardened. If at any point, the ice cream is too hard to beat, place it in the refrigerator until it becomes soft enough to beat.
5. In the last churning add the crushed chocolate mint candies and beat the ice cream one last time, so the chocolate mint candies will spread evenly.

6. Serve right away or transfer the ice cream to an airtight freezer-safe container.

Nutrition per Serving
Calories 397, fat 26 g, carbs 32 g, sugar 73 g
Protein 2 g, sodium 35 mg

Vanilla Cheesecake Ice Cream

Makes about 5 cups (½ cup per serving)

Ingredients

12 ounces cream cheese, softened
1 cup whole milk
¼ cup mascarpone
1 cup granulated sugar
1 teaspoon vanilla extract
¼ cup sour cream

Directions

With an ice cream maker

1. Freeze the ice cream maker bowl according to manufacturer instructions, usually 12 to 24 hours.
2. Meanwhile, add the cream cheese in a high-speed blender. Blend the cream until very smooth.
3. Pour in the sugar little by little. Blend until the mixture is creamy and sugar dissolves.
4. While the blender is still running, pour the milk, vanilla, and mascarpone slowly. Transfer the mixture into a clean bowl, preferably with a spout, and fold the sour cream.
5. Cover with a plastic wrap and let the mixture cool in the refrigerator for at least 2 to 12 hours.
6. Pull out the ice cream mixture from the refrigerator and stir a few times.
7. Install the frozen ice cream maker bowl and pour the mixture into it.
8. Connect the machine and press ice cream and the start button.
9. When the cycle is finished, transfer the ice cream to an airtight freezer-safe container or serve right away. The ice cream will be soft and creamy. If you like a harder texture, allow the ice cream to freeze for 2 hours or more before serving.

Without an ice cream maker

1. Add the cream cheese in a high-speed blender. Blend the cream until very smooth. Pour in the sugar little by little. Blend until the mixture is creamy and sugar dissolves.
2. While the blender is still running, pour the milk, vanilla, and mascarpone slowly. Pour the mixture in a Pyrex or stainless steel 9x13-inch pan and fold the sour cream.
3. Place it in the freezer for 30 minutes. The edges should start freezing. Using an electric handheld mixer, beat the ice cream for 1 minute.
4. Return to the freezer for another 30 minutes and beat again as before. Do this same step 4-5 times until the ice cream has hardened. If at any point, the ice cream is too hard to beat, place it in the refrigerator until it becomes soft enough to beat.

5. In the last churning add the crushed chocolate mint candies and beat the ice cream one last time, so the chocolate mint candies will spread evenly.
6. Serve right away or transfer the ice cream to an airtight freezer-safe container.

Nutrition per Serving
Calories 240, fat 15 g, carbs 23 g, sugar 63 g
Protein 4 g, sodium 45 mg

GELATO RECIPES

Lemon Gelato

Makes about 4 cups (½ cup per serving)

Ingredients
1 cup whole milk
1 cup granulated sugar
3 tablespoons grated lemon zest
¾ cup lemon juice
1 cup heavy cream

Directions
With an ice cream maker

1. Freeze the ice cream maker bowl according to manufacturer instructions, usually 12 to 24 hours.
2. Meanwhile in a saucepan, warm the whole milk, the granulated sugar, and lemon zest over medium heat. Stir until the sugar is fully dissolved. Bring the mixture to a soft simmer for about 10 to 12 minutes.
3. Pour into a clean bowl, preferably with a spout, and set aside. Stir in the lemon juice and heavy cream. Mix until combined. Let the mixture cool at room temperature.
4. Cover with a plastic wrap and let the mixture cool in the refrigerator for at least 2 to 12 hours.
5. Pull out the gelato mixture from the refrigerator and stir a few times.
6. Install the frozen ice cream maker bowl and pour the gelato mixture into it.
7. Connect the machine and press gelato and the start button.
8. When the cycle is finished, transfer the gelato to an airtight freezer-safe container or serve right away. The gelato will be soft and creamy. If you like a harder texture, allow the gelato to freeze for 2 hours or more before serving.

Without an ice cream maker

1. In a saucepan, warm the whole milk, the granulated sugar, and lemon zest over medium heat. Stir until the sugar is fully dissolved. Bring the mixture to a soft simmer for about 10 to 12 minutes.
2. Pour into a clean bowl, preferably with a spout, and set aside. Stir in the lemon juice and heavy cream. Mix until combined.
3. Let the mixture cool at room temperature.
4. Pour the mixture in a Pyrex or stainless steel 9x13-inch pan. And place in the freezer for 30 minutes. The edges should start freezing. Using an electric handheld mixer, beat the gelato for 1 minute.

5. Return to the freezer for another 30 minutes and beat again as before. Do this same step 4-5 times until the gelato is harder. If at any point, the gelato is too hard to beat, place it in the refrigerator until it becomes soft enough to beat.
6. Serve right away or transfer the gelato to an airtight freezer-safe container.

Nutrition per Serving

Calories 341, fat 14 g, carbs 56 g, sugar 55 g
Protein 3 g, sodium 45 mg

Biscotti Gelato

Makes about 4 cups (½ cup per serving)

Ingredients

2 cups whole milk
1 cup heavy cream
¾ cup granulated sugar
2 tablespoons honey
1 teaspoon almond extract
½ cup crushed biscotti cookies

Directions

With an ice cream maker

1. Freeze the ice cream maker bowl according to manufacturer instructions, usually 12 to 24 hours.
2. Meanwhile in a medium saucepan, warm the whole milk, the granulated sugar, and honey over medium heat until the sugar and honey are fully dissolved.
3. Remove pan from the heat and stir in the almond extract and heavy cream. Mix until combined.
4. Pour the mixture in a clean bowl, preferably with a spout, and let it cool at room temperature.
5. Cover with a plastic wrap and let the mixture cool in the refrigerator for at least 2 to 12 hours.
6. Pull out the gelato mixture from the refrigerator and stir a few times.
7. Install the frozen ice cream maker bowl and pour the gelato mixture into it.
8. Connect the machine and press gelato and the start button.
9. About 5 minutes before then end of the churning process, add the crushed biscotti cookies little by little into the gelato and let it mix in.
10. When the cycle is finished, transfer the gelato to an airtight freezer-safe container or serve right away. The gelato will be soft and creamy. If you like a harder texture, allow the gelato to freeze for 2 hours or more before serving.

Without an ice cream maker

1. In a medium saucepan, heat the whole milk, the granulated sugar, and honey over medium heat until the sugar and honey are fully dissolved.
2. Remove pan from the heat and stir in the almond extract and heavy cream. Mix until combined.
3. Pour the mixture in a clean bowl and let it cool at room temperature.
4. Pour the mixture in a Pyrex or stainless steel 9x13-inch pan. And place in the freezer for 30 minutes. The edges should start freezing. Using an electric handheld mixer, beat the gelato for 1 minute.

5. Return to the freezer for another 30 minutes and beat again as before. Do this same step 4-5 times until the gelato is harder. If at any point, the gelato is too hard to beat, place it in the refrigerator until it becomes soft enough to beat.
6. In the last churning add the crushed biscotti cookies and beat the gelato one last time, so the biscotti will spread evenly.
7. Serve right away or transfer the gelato to an airtight freezer-safe container.

Nutrition per Serving

Calories 412, fat 17 g, carbs 64 g, sugar 56 g
Protein 6 g, sodium 86 mg

Panna Cotta Gelato

Makes about 4 cups (½ cup per serving)

Ingredients
2 ¼ cups whole milk
1 cup heavy cream
⅔ cup granulated sugar
1 teaspoon vanilla extract

Directions

With an ice cream maker

1. Freeze the ice cream maker bowl according to manufacturer instructions, usually 12 to 24 hours.
2. Meanwhile in a medium saucepan, warm the whole milk, heavy cream, and the granulated sugar over medium heat, about 10 to 12 minutes.
3. Simmer until the whole sugar is dissolved. Stir continuously until the mixture thickens. The best way to know when it is ready is when the mixture coats the back of a spoon.
4. Remove pan from heat and stir in the vanilla extract. Mix until combined.
5. Pour the whole mixture in a clean bowl, preferably with a spout, and let cool to room temperature.
6. Cover with a plastic wrap and let the mixture cool in the refrigerator for at least 2 to 12 hours.
7. Pull out the gelato mixture from the refrigerator and stir a few times.
8. Install the frozen ice cream maker bowl and pour the gelato mixture into it.
9. Connect the machine and press gelato and the start button.
10. When the cycle is finished, transfer the gelato to an airtight freezer-safe container or serve right away. The gelato will be soft and creamy. If you like a harder texture, allow the gelato to freeze for 2 hours or more before serving.

Without an ice cream maker

1. In a medium saucepan, warm the whole milk, heavy cream, and the granulated sugar over medium heat, about 10 to 12 minutes.
2. Simmer until the whole sugar is dissolved. Stir continuously until the mixture thickens. The best way to know when it is ready is when the mixture coats the back of a spoon.
3. Remove pan from heat and stir in the vanilla extract. Mix until combined.
4. Pour the whole mixture in a clean bowl, preferably with a spout, and let cool to room temperature.
5. Pour the mixture in a Pyrex or stainless steel 9x13-inch pan and place it in the freezer for 30 minutes. The edges should start freezing. Using an electric handheld mix, beat the gelato for 1 minute.

6. Return to the freezer for another 30 minutes and beat again as before. Do this same step 4-5 times until the gelato is harder. If at any point, the gelato is too hard to beat, place it in the refrigerator until it becomes soft enough to beat.
7. Serve right away or transfer the gelato to an airtight freezer-safe container.

Nutrition per Serving

Calories 314, fat 16 g, carbs 41 g, sugar 4 g
Protein 5 g, sodium 66 mg

Creamy Pistachio Gelato

Makes about 4 cups (½ cup per serving)

Ingredients
2 cups whole milk
1 cup heavy cream
¾ cup granulated sugar
1 teaspoon vanilla extract
6 tablespoons pistachio paste

Directions
With an ice cream maker

1. Freeze the ice cream maker bowl according to manufacturer instructions, usually 12 to 24 hours.
2. Meanwhile in a medium saucepan, warm the whole milk, the heavy cream, and the granulated sugar over medium-low heat.
3. Simmer until the sugar is completely dissolved. Stir continuously until the mixture thickens, about 15-20 minutes. The best way to know when it is ready is when the mixture coats the back of a spoon.
4. Remove from heat, stir in the vanilla extract and pistachio paste. Mix until combined and smooth. Transfer to a clean bowl, preferably with a spout.
5. Cover with plastic wrap and place in the refrigerator for at least 2 hours to 12 hours.
6. Pull out the gelato mixture from the refrigerator and stir a few times.
7. Install the frozen ice cream maker bowl and pour the mixture into the ice cream maker. Connect the machine and press gelato and the start button.
8. When the cycle is finished, transfer the gelato to an airtight freezer-safe container or serve right away. The gelato will be soft and creamy. If you like a harder texture, allow the gelato to freeze for 2 hours or more before serving.

Without an ice cream maker

1. In a medium saucepan, heat the whole milk, the heavy cream, and the granulated sugar over medium-low heat.
2. Simmer until the sugar is completely dissolved, about 15-20 minutes. Stir continuously until the mixture thickens. The best way to know when it is ready is when the mixture coats the back of a spoon.
3. Remove pan from heat, stir in the vanilla extract and pistachio paste. Mix until combined and smooth.
4. Pour the mixture in a Pyrex or stainless steel 9x13-inch pan and place it in the freezer for 30 minutes. The edges should start freezing. Using an electric handheld mixer, beat the gelato for 1 minute.

5. Return to the freezer for another 30 minutes and beat again as before. Do this same step 4-5 times until the gelato has hardened. If at any point, the gelato becomes too hard to beat, place it in the refrigerator until it becomes soft enough to beat.
6. Serve right away or transfer the gelato to an airtight freezer-safe container.

Nutrition per Serving

Calories 448, fat 25 g, carbs 53 g, sugar 50 g
Protein 8 g, sodium 68 mg

Strawberry Gelato

Makes about 4 cups (½ cup per serving)

Ingredients

2 cups whole milk
½ cup heavy cream
¾ cup icing sugar
3 tablespoons light corn syrup
1 teaspoon vanilla extract
1 teaspoon lemon juice
2 ½ cups chopped strawberries

Directions

With an ice cream maker

1. Freeze the ice cream maker bowl according to manufacturer instructions, usually 12 to 24 hours.
2. Meanwhile in a high-speed blender or food processor, add the whole milk, heavy cream, icing sugar, light corn syrup, vanilla extract, lemon juice, and chopped strawberries.
3. Blitz until everything is combined and smooth mixture develops.
4. Transfer the gelato base into a clean bowl, preferably with a spout.
5. Cover with a plastic wrap and let the mixture cool in the refrigerator for at least 2 to 12 hours.
6. Pull out the gelato mixture from the refrigerator and stir a few times.
7. Install the frozen ice cream maker bowl and pour the gelato mixture into it.
8. Connect the machine and press gelato and the start button.
9. When the cycle is finished, transfer the gelato to an airtight freezer-safe container or serve right away. The gelato will be soft and creamy. If you like a harder texture, allow the gelato to freeze for 2 hours or more before serving.

Without an ice cream maker

1. In a high-speed blender or food processor, add the whole milk, heavy cream, icing sugar, light corn syrup, vanilla extract, lemon juice, and chopped strawberries.
2. Blitz until everything is combined and smooth mixture develops.
3. Transfer the gelato base into a clean bowl, preferably with a spout.
4. Pour the mixture in a Pyrex or stainless steel 9x13-inch pan. And place in the freezer for 30 minutes. The edges should start freezing. Using an electric handheld mixer, beat the gelato for 1 minute.
5. Return to the freezer for another 30 minutes and beat again as before. Do this same step 4-5 times until the gelato is harder. If at any point, the gelato is too hard to beat, place it in the refrigerator until it becomes soft enough to beat.
6. Serve right away or transfer the gelato to an airtight freezer-safe container.

Nutrition per Serving
Calories 285, fat 10 g, carbs 46 g, sugar 37 g
Protein 5 g, sodium 56 mg

Hazelnut Gelato

Makes about 4 cups (½ cup per serving)

Ingredients

2 cups whole milk
1 cup heavy cream
2/3 cup granulated sugar
1 teaspoon vanilla extract
1 teaspoon hazelnut extract
6 tablespoons hazelnut butter

Directions

With an ice cream maker

1. Freeze the ice cream maker bowl according to manufacturer instructions, usually 12 to 24 hours.
2. Meanwhile, in a medium saucepan, warm the whole milk with the granulated sugar on medium heat.
3. Simmer until it reaches almost to a boiling point and the whole sugar is dissolved, about 15-20 minutes.
4. Remove from heat and stir in the vanilla extract, hazelnut extract, and hazelnut butter. Mix until combined and smooth, then stir in the heavy cream.
5. Pour the whole mixture in a clean bowl, preferably with a spout, and let cool to room temperature.
6. Cover with a plastic wrap and let the mixture cool in the refrigerator for at least 2 to 12 hours.
7. Pull out the gelato mixture from the refrigerator and stir a few times.
8. Install the frozen ice cream maker bowl and pour the gelato mixture into it.
9. Connect the machine and press gelato and the start button.
10. When the cycle is finished, transfer the gelato to an airtight freezer-safe container or serve right away. The gelato will be soft and creamy. If you like a harder texture, allow the gelato to freeze for 2 hours or more before serving.

Without an ice cream maker

1. In a medium saucepan, heat the whole milk with the granulated sugar on medium heat.
2. Simmer until it reaches almost to a boiling point and the whole sugar is dissolved, about 15 to 20 minutes.
3. Remove from heat and stir in the vanilla extract, hazelnut extract, and hazelnut butter. Mix until combined and smooth and then stir in the heavy cream.
4. Pour the whole mixture in a clean bowl, preferably with a spout, and let cool to room temperature.

5. Pour the mixture in a Pyrex or stainless steel 9x13-inch pan. And place in the freezer for 30 minutes. The edges should start freezing. Using an electric handheld mixer, beat the gelato for 1 minute.
6. Return to the freezer for another 30 minutes and beat again as before. Do this same step 4-5 times until the gelato is harder. If at any point, the gelato is too hard to beat, place it in the refrigerator until it becomes soft enough to beat.
7. Serve right away or transfer the gelato to an airtight freezer-safe container.

Nutrition per Serving

Calories 477, fat 32 g, carbs 41 g, sugar 41 g
Protein 9 g, sodium 62 mg

Mango Gelato

Makes about 5 cups (½ cup per serving)

Ingredients

2 ½ cups whole milk
1 cup heavy cream
2 pound very ripe mango diced into cubes
2/3 cup icing sugar
1 teaspoon vanilla extract

Directions

With an ice cream maker

1. Freeze the ice cream maker bowl according to manufacturer instructions, usually 12 to 24 hours.
2. Meanwhile in a high-speed blender, add the milk, ripe mango cubes, and the icing sugar.
3. Blitz until creamy and smooth. If you have smaller blender do this in two or three batches so the gelato base can be evenly blended into a smoother texture.
4. Transfer the mango puree in a clean bowl, preferably with a spout, and stir in the heavy cream and vanilla extract.
5. Cover with a plastic wrap and let the mixture cool in the refrigerator for at least 2 to 12 hours.
6. Pull out the gelato mixture from the refrigerator and stir a few times.
7. Install the frozen ice cream maker bowl and pour the gelato mixture into it.
8. Connect the machine and press gelato and the start button.
9. When the cycle is finished, transfer the gelato to an airtight freezer-safe container or serve right away. The gelato will be soft and creamy. If you like a harder texture, allow the gelato to freeze for 2 hours or more before serving.

Without an ice cream maker

1. In a high-speed blender, add the milk, ripe mango cubes, and the icing sugar.
2. Blitz until creamy and smooth. If you have smaller blender do this in two or three batches so the gelato base can be evenly blended into a smoother texture.
3. Transfer the mango puree in a clean bowl, preferably with a spout, and stir in the heavy cream and vanilla extract.
4. Pour the mixture in a Pyrex or stainless steel 9x13-inch pan. And place in the freezer for 30 minutes. The edges should start freezing. Using an electric handheld mixer, beat the gelato for 1 minute.
5. Return to the freezer for another 30 minutes and beat again as before. Do this same step 4-5 times until the gelato is harder. If at any point, the gelato is too hard to beat, place it in the refrigerator until it becomes soft enough to beat.
6. Serve right away or transfer the gelato to an airtight freezer-safe container.

Nutrition per Serving
Calories 412, fat 17 g, carbs 62 g, sugar 59 g
Protein 7 g, sodium 75 mg

Vanilla Gelato

Makes about 4 cups (½ cup per serving)

Ingredients

2 ½ cups whole milk
7 egg yolks
½ cup heavy cream
1 cup granulated sugar
1 tablespoon vanilla extract

Directions

With an ice cream maker

1. Freeze the ice cream maker bowl according to manufacturer instructions, usually 12 to 24 hours.
2. Meanwhile, warm the milk, heavy cream, and sugar in a saucepan over medium heat. Bring the mixture to a soft simmer for about 15 to 20 minutes. Set aside.
3. In another bowl, whisk the egg yolks and pour the hot milk mixture over it. Whisk constantly so you won't end up with scrambled eggs.
4. Stir in the vanilla.
5. Pour the mixture back into the saucepan and heat the whole mixture again over medium heat until it gets a smooth and creamy texture.
6. Strain the gelato base into a clean bowl, preferably with a spout, over a fine-mesh sieve so you will ensure that there are no small pieces of the egg yolks.
7. Cover with a plastic wrap and let the mixture cool in the refrigerator for at least 2 to 12 hours.
8. Pull out the gelato mixture from the refrigerator and stir a few times.
9. Install the frozen ice cream maker bowl and pour the gelato mixture into it.
10. Connect the machine and press gelato and the start button.
11. When the cycle is finished, transfer the gelato to an airtight freezer-safe container or serve right away. The gelato will be soft and creamy. If you like a harder texture, allow the gelato to freeze for 2 hours or more before serving.

Without an ice cream maker

1. Warm the milk, heavy cream, and sugar in a saucepan over medium heat. Bring the mixture to a soft simmer for about 15 to 20 minutes. Set aside.
2. In another bowl, whisk the egg yolks and pour the hot milk mixture over it. Whisk constantly so you won't end up with scrambled eggs.
3. Stir in the vanilla.
4. Pour the mixture back into the saucepan and heat the whole mixture again over medium heat until it gets a smooth and creamy texture.
5. Strain the gelato base into a clean bowl, preferably with a spout, over a fine-mesh sieve so you will ensure that there are no small pieces of the egg yolks.

6. Pour the mixture in a Pyrex or stainless steel 9x13-inch pan. And place in the freezer for 30 minutes. The edges should start freezing. Using an electric handheld mixer, beat the gelato for 1 minute.
7. Return to the freezer for another 30 minutes and beat again as before. Do this same step 4-5 times until the gelato is harder. If at any point, the gelato is too hard to beat, place it in the refrigerator until it becomes soft enough to beat.
8. Serve right away or transfer the gelato to an airtight freezer-safe container.

Nutrition per Serving

Calories 434, fat 18 g, carbs 59 g, sugar 59 g
Protein 10 g, sodium 81 mg

Chocolate Gelato

Makes about 4 cups (½ cup per serving)

Ingredients

3 cups whole milk
5 oz. bittersweet chocolate, chopped into smaller pieces
¼ cup cocoa powder
1 cup granulated sugar
2 tablespoons instant chocolate pudding

Directions

With an ice cream maker

1. Freeze the ice cream maker bowl according to manufacturer instructions, usually 12 to 24 hours.
2. Meanwhile in a saucepan, heat 2 cups of the whole milk over medium-low heat.
3. Bring the mixture to a soft simmer for about 15 to 20 minutes then remove from heat. Stir in the chopped bittersweet chocolate. Let it melt all the way through.
4. In another saucepan, heat 1 cup of the whole milk, stir in the sugar, cocoa powder, and instant chocolate pudding over medium-low heat.
5. Combine the two mixtures together and heat the whole mixture again over medium-low heat and cook until thickens.
6. Remove from heat and transfer the gelato base in a clean bowl, preferably with a spout.
7. Cover with a plastic wrap and let the mixture cool in the refrigerator for at least 2 to 12 hours.
8. Pull out the gelato mixture from the refrigerator and stir a few times.
9. Install the frozen ice cream maker bowl and pour the gelato mixture into it.
10. Connect the machine and press gelato and the start button.
11. When the cycle is finished, transfer the gelato to an airtight freezer-safe container or serve right away. The gelato will be soft and creamy. If you like a harder texture, allow the gelato to freeze for 2 hours or more before serving.

Without an ice cream maker

1. In a saucepan, heat 2 cups of the whole milk over medium-low heat.
2. Bring the mixture to a soft simmer for about 15 to 20 minutes then remove from heat. Stir in the chopped bittersweet chocolate. Let it melt all the way through.
3. In another saucepan, heat 1 cup of the whole milk, stir in the sugar, cocoa powder, and instant chocolate pudding over medium-low heat.
4. Combine the two mixtures together and heat the whole mixture again over medium-low heat and cook until thickens.
5. Remove from heat and transfer the gelato base in a clean bowl, preferably with a spout.

6. Pour the mixture in a Pyrex or stainless steel 9x13-inch pan. And place in the freezer for 30 minutes. The edges should start freezing. Using an electric handheld mixer, beat the gelato for 1 minute.
7. Return to the freezer for another 30 minutes and beat again as before. Do this same step 4-5 times until the gelato is harder. If at any point, the gelato is too hard to beat, place it in the refrigerator until it becomes soft enough to beat.
8. Serve right away or transfer the gelato to an airtight freezer-safe container.

Nutrition per Serving

Calories 511, fat 17 g, carbs 85 g, sugar 78 g
Protein 10 g, sodium 252 mg

Caramel Gelato

Makes about 4 cups (½ cup per serving)

Ingredients

2 cups whole milk
1 cup heavy cream
1 teaspoon salt
7 egg yolks
1 cup granulated sugar
½ cup caramel

Directions

With an ice cream maker

1. Freeze the ice cream maker bowl according to manufacturer instructions, usually 12 to 24 hours.
2. Meanwhile, warm the milk and heavy cream in a saucepan over medium-low heat. Bring the mixture to a soft simmer for about 15 to 20 minutes. Set aside.
3. In another bowl, whisk the egg yolks with the sugar and pour the hot milk mixture over it. Whisk constantly so you won't end up cooking the egg yolks.
4. Pour the mixture back into the saucepan and heat the whole mixture again over medium-low heat until creamy and thickened. You know it's ready when the mixture coats the back of a spoon.
5. Strain the gelato base in a clean bowl, preferably with a spout, over a fine-mesh sieve to strain any cooked pieces of egg yolks.
6. In a clean bowl, mix the salt and the caramel. Pour it into the gelato base.
7. Cover with a plastic wrap and let the mixture cool in the refrigerator for at least 2 to 12 hours.
8. Pull out the gelato mixture from the refrigerator and stir a few times.
9. Install the frozen ice cream maker bowl and pour the gelato mixture into it.
10. Connect the machine and press gelato and the start button.
11. When the cycle is finished, transfer the gelato to an airtight freezer-safe container or serve right away. The gelato will be soft and creamy. If you like a harder texture, allow the gelato to freeze for 2 hours or more before serving.

Without an ice cream maker

1. Warm the milk and heavy cream in a saucepan over medium-low heat. Bring the mixture to a soft simmer for about 15 to 20 minutes. Set aside.
2. In another bowl, whisk the egg yolks with the sugar and pour the hot milk mixture over it. Whisk constantly so you won't end up cooking the egg yolks.
3. Pour the mixture back into the saucepan and heat the whole mixture again over medium-low heat until creamy and thickened. You know it's ready when the mixture coats the back of a spoon.

4. Strain the gelato base in a clean bowl, preferably with a spout, over a fine-mesh sieve to strain any cooked pieces of egg yolks.
5. In a clean bowl, mix the salt and the caramel. Pour it into the gelato base.
6. Pour the mixture in a Pyrex or stainless steel 9x13-inch pan and place it in the freezer for 30 minutes. The edges should start freezing. Using an electric handheld mixer, beat the gelato for 1 minute.
7. Return to the freezer for another 30 minutes and beat again as before. Do this same step 4-5 times until the gelato is harder. If at any point, the gelato is too hard to beat, place it in the refrigerator until it becomes soft enough to beat.
8. Serve right away or transfer the gelato to an airtight freezer-safe container and store it in the freezer until you are ready to use it.

Nutrition per Serving

Calories 496, fat 24 g, carbs 64 g, sugar 57 g
Protein 10 g, sodium 680 mg

Toasted Butter Pecan Gelato

Makes about 4 cups (½ cup per serving)

Ingredients

2 cups whole milk
1 cup heavy cream
¾ cup light brown sugar
5 egg yolks
pinch of salt
1 teaspoon vanilla extract
2 tablespoons butter
1 cup toasted pecans, chopped

Directions

With an ice cream maker

1. Freeze the ice cream maker bowl according to manufacturer instructions, usually 12 to 24 hours.
2. Meanwhile in a saucepan, add the whole milk, heavy cream, and the light brown sugar over medium heat. Mix to combine completely. Bring the mixture to a soft simmer for about 10 to 12 minutes. Set aside.
3. Add the egg yolks in a clean bowl. Pour the hot milk mixture into it slowly while constantly whisking to temper the egg yolks so you won't end up with scrambled eggs.
4. Pour the mixture back into the saucepan and heat the whole mixture again over medium-low heat until creamy and thickened. You know it's ready when the mixture coats the back of a spoon.
5. Strain the mixture into a clean bowl over a fine-mesh sieve to remove all cooked pieces of the egg yolks. Discard.
6. Stir in the salt and the vanilla extract. Mix until everything is well incorporated.
7. Cover the mixture with plastic wrap and let the mixture cool in the refrigerator for at least 2 to 12 hours.
8. Meanwhile, melt the butter in a skillet over medium-low heat and toast the pecans for 5 minutes while constantly stirring them.
9. Scoop the pecans out of the butter and let them cool completely.
10. Pull out the gelato mixture from the refrigerator and stir a few times.
11. Install the frozen ice cream maker bowl and pour the gelato mixture into it.
12. Connect the machine and press gelato and the start button.
13. About 5-6 minutes before the end of the churning process, add the chopped pecans little by little into the gelato and let it mix in.
14. When the cycle is finished, transfer the gelato to an airtight freezer-safe container or serve right away. The gelato will be soft and creamy. If you like a harder texture, allow the gelato to freeze for 2 hours or more before serving.

Without an ice cream maker

1. In a saucepan, add the whole milk, heavy cream, and the light brown sugar over medium heat. Mix to combine completely. Bring the mixture to a soft simmer for about 10 to 12 minutes. Set aside.
2. Add the egg yolks in a clean bowl. Pour the hot milk mixture into it slowly while constantly whisking to temper the egg yolks so you won't end up with scrambled eggs.
3. Pour the mixture back into the saucepan and heat the whole mixture again over medium-low heat until creamy and thickened. You know it's ready when the mixture coats the back of a spoon.
4. Strain the mixture into a clean bowl over a fine-mesh sieve to remove all cooked pieces of the egg yolks. Discard.
5. Stir in the salt and the vanilla extract. Mix until everything is well incorporated.
6. Meanwhile, melt the butter over medium-low heat in a skillet and toast the pecans for 5 minutes while constantly stirring them.
7. Scoop pecans out of the butter and let them cool completely.
8. Pour the mixture in a Pyrex or stainless steel 9x13-inch pan and place it in the freezer for 30 minutes. The edges should start freezing. Using an electric handheld mixer, beat the gelato for 1 minute.
9. Return to the freezer for another 30 minutes and beat again as before. Do this same step 4-5 times until the gelato has hardened. If at any point, the gelato is too hard to beat, place it in the refrigerator until it becomes soft enough to beat.
10. In the last churning add the pecans and beat the gelato one last time, so the pecans will spread evenly.
11. Serve right away or transfer the gelato to an airtight freezer-safe container.

Nutrition per Serving

Calories 575, fat 44 g, carbs 38 g, sugar 34 g
Protein 11 g, sodium 158 mg

Pineapple and Coconut Gelato

Makes about 4 cups (½ cup per serving)

Ingredients
2 cups whole milk
½ cup heavy cream
1 cup granulated sugar
1 ¼ cups toasted coconut flakes*
½ cup fresh pineapple, diced thin or ½ (8-ounce) can crushed pineapple drained
5 egg yolks
1 teaspoon vanilla extract

Directions
<u>With an ice cream maker</u>

1. Freeze the ice cream maker bowl according to manufacturer instructions, usually 12 to 24 hours.
2. Meanwhile in a saucepan, heat the milk, heavy cream, granulated sugar, and toasted coconut flakes over medium heat. Bring the mixture to a soft simmer for about 15 to 20 minutes. Set aside.
3. Add the egg yolks in a bowl, pour the hot milk mixture slowly into it while whisking constantly so you won't end up with scrambled eggs.
4. Pour the mixture back into the saucepan and heat the whole mixture again over medium-low heat until creamy and thickened. You know it's ready when the mixture coats the back of a spoon.
5. Pour the mixture in a clean bowl over a fine-mesh sieve to strain and remove any cooked pieces of the egg yolks. Let it cool to room temperature.
6. Cover with a plastic wrap and let the mixture cool in the refrigerator for at least 2 to 12 hours.
7. Pull out the gelato mixture from the refrigerator and stir a few times.
8. Install the frozen ice cream maker bowl and pour the mixture into it.
9. Connect the machine and press gelato and the start button.
10. About 5 minutes before then end of the churning process, add the pineapple and 1 cup toasted coconut little by little into the gelato and let them mix in.
11. When the cycle is finished, transfer the gelato to an airtight freezer-safe container or serve right away. The gelato will be soft and creamy. If you like a harder texture, allow the gelato to freeze for 2 hours or more before serving.
12. To serve, top with a sprinkle of toasted coconut.

<u>Without an ice cream maker</u>

1. In a saucepan, heat the milk, heavy cream, granulated sugar, and toasted coconut flakes over medium heat. Bring the mixture to a soft simmer for about 15 to 20 minutes. Set aside.

2. Add the egg yolks in a bowl, pour the hot milk mixture slowly into it while whisking constantly so you won't end up with scrambled eggs.
3. Pour the mixture back into the saucepan and heat the whole mixture again over medium-low heat until creamy and thickened. You know it's ready when the mixture coats the back of a spoon.
4. Pour the mixture in a clean bowl over a fine-mesh sieve to strain and remove any cooked pieces of the egg yolks. Let it cool to room temperature.
5. Pour the mixture in a Pyrex or stainless steel 9x13-inch pan. And place in the freezer for 30 minutes. The edges should start freezing. Using an electric handheld mixer, beat the gelato for 1 minute.
6. Return to the freezer for another 30 minutes and beat again as before. Do this same step 4-5 times until the gelato has hardened. If at any point, the gelato is too hard to beat, place it in the refrigerator until it becomes soft enough to beat.
7. In the last churning add the pineapple and 1 cup of toasted coconut. Beat the gelato one last time, so the cherries and almonds spread evenly.
8. Serve right away with an extra sprinkle of toasted coconut or transfer the gelato to an airtight freezer-safe container.

* To toast the coconut flakes, preheat oven to 350^{0}F. Evenly spread the coconut flakes on a baking sheet lined with parchment paper or a silicone mat. Bake for 10-15 minutes. Toss the coconut with a spatula every 5 minutes, taking care of watching not to let the coconut flakes burn too much. Let cool down before using it. Store in an airtight container.

Nutrition per Serving
Calories 454, fat 22 g, carbs 60 g, sugar 58 g, protein 8 g, sodium 69 mg

Cherry and Almond Gelato

Makes about 4 cups (½ cup per serving)

Ingredients

2 cups whole milk
1 (14-ounce). can sweetened condensed milk
¼ cup heavy cream
2 teaspoons vanilla extract
1 cup pitted and chopped fresh cherries
¼ cup almonds, roughly chopped
2 tablespoons cherry liquor

Directions

With an ice cream maker

1. Freeze the ice cream maker bowl according to manufacturer instructions, usually 12 to 24 hours.
2. Meanwhile in a large bowl, add the whole milk, condensed milk, heavy cream, vanilla extract, and cherry liquor. Whisk until everything is combined and smooth.
3. Cover the mixture with plastic wrap and let the mixture cool in the refrigerator for at least 2 to 12 hours.
4. Pull out the gelato mixture from the refrigerator and stir a few times.
5. Install the frozen ice cream maker bowl and pour the mixture into it.
6. Connect the machine and press gelato and the start button.
7. About 5 to 6 minutes before then end of the churning process, add the chopped cherries and almonds little by little into the gelato and let them mix in.
8. When the cycle is finished, transfer the gelato to an airtight freezer-safe container or serve right away. The gelato will be soft and creamy. If you like a harder texture, allow the gelato to freeze for 2 hours or more before serving.

Without an ice cream maker

1. In a large bowl, add the whole milk, condensed milk, heavy cream, vanilla extract, and cherry liquor. Whisk until everything is combined and smooth.
2. Pour the mixture in a Pyrex or stainless steel 9x13-inch pan and place it in the freezer for 30 minutes. The edges should start freezing. Using an electric handheld mixer, beat the gelato for 1 minute.
3. Return to the freezer for another 30 minutes and beat again as before. Do this same step 4-5 times until the gelato has hardened. If at any point, the gelato is too hard to beat, place it in the refrigerator until it becomes soft enough to beat.
4. In the last churning add the chopped cherries and almonds. Beat the gelato one last time, so the cherries and almonds spread evenly.
5. Serve right away or transfer the gelato to an airtight freezer-safe container.

Nutrition per Serving
Calories 443, fat 20 g, carbs 65 g, sugar 64 g, protein 13 g, sodium 178 mg

Nutella Gelato

Makes about 4 cups (½ cup per serving)

Ingredients

2 cups whole milk
1 cup heavy cream
½ cup granulated sugar
4 egg yolks
1 teaspoon vanilla extract
6 tablespoons chocolate hazelnut spread like Nutella

Directions

With an ice cream maker

1. Freeze the ice cream maker bowl according to manufacturer instructions, usually 12 to 24 hours.
2. Meanwhile, in a saucepan, warm the whole milk and heavy cream with the granulated sugar over medium heat. Bring the mixture to a soft simmer for about 15 to 20 minutes. Set aside.
3. In a clean bowl, add the egg yolks and whisk. Start pouring slowly the warm milk mixture into it to temper your egg yolks so you won't end up with scrambled eggs.
4. Pour the mixture back into the saucepan and heat again over medium-low heat until creamy and thickened. You know it's ready when the mixture coats the back of a spoon.
5. Remove from the heat. Stir in the vanilla extract and chocolate hazelnut spread. Mix until combined and smooth.
6. Cover with a plastic wrap and let the mixture cool in the refrigerator for at least 2 to 12 hours.
7. Meanwhile, chop up the hazelnuts and toast them in a nonstick frying pan on medium heat for about 2-3 minutes, stir constantly. Set aside for later use.
8. Pull out the gelato mixture from the refrigerator and stir a few times.
9. Install the frozen ice cream maker bowl and pour the mixture into it.
10. Connect the machine and press gelato and the start button.
11. When the cycle is finished, transfer the gelato to an airtight freezer-safe container or serve right away. The gelato will be soft and creamy. If you like a harder texture, allow the gelato to freeze for 2 hours or more before serving.

Without an ice cream maker

1. In a saucepan, warm the whole milk and heavy cream with the granulated sugar over medium heat. Bring the mixture to a soft simmer for about 15 to 20 minutes. Set aside.
2. In a clean bowl, add the egg yolks and whisk. Start pouring slowly the warm milk mixture into it to temper your egg yolks so you won't end up with scrambled eggs.

3. Pour the mixture back into the saucepan and heat again over medium-low heat until creamy and thickened. You know it's ready when the mixture coats the back of a spoon.
4. Remove from the heat. Stir in the vanilla extract and chocolate hazelnut spread. Mix until combined and smooth.
5. Meanwhile, chop up the hazelnuts and toast them in a nonstick frying pan on medium heat for about 2-3 minutes, stir constantly. Set aside for later use.
6. Pour the gelato mixture in a Pyrex or stainless steel 9x13-inch pan. And place in the freezer for 30 minutes. The edges should start freezing. Using an electric handheld mixer, beat the gelato for 1 minute.
7. Return to the freezer for another 30 minutes and beat again as before. Do this same step 4-5 times until the gelato is harder. If at any point, the gelato is too hard to beat, place it in the refrigerator until it becomes soft enough to beat.
8. Serve right away or transfer the gelato to an airtight freezer-safe container.

Nutrition per Serving

Calories 529, fat 34.3 g, carbs 48.7 g, sugar 46.3 g
Protein 10.3 g, sodium 83 mg

SHERBET RECIPES

Orange Sherbet

Makes about 4 cups (½ cup per serving)

Ingredients

1 cup granulated sugar
zest of 1 orange
2 cups freshly squeezed orange juice
1 teaspoon vanilla extract
1 cup chilled heavy cream
½ cup chilled whole milk

Directions

With an ice cream maker

1. Freeze the ice cream maker bowl according to manufacturer instructions, usually 12 to 24 hours.
2. Meanwhile, place the granulated sugar, orange juice, and zest and vanilla extract in a high-speed blender or food processor.
3. Blitz until everything is combined and well incorporated and the sugar is fully dissolved.
4. Transfer the mixture into a clean bowl, preferably with a spout, and stir in the heavy cream and whole milk. Mix until everything is combined.
5. Cover with plastic wrap and let it chill in the fridge for a minimum of 2 to 12 hours. Pull out the sherbet mixture from the refrigerator and stir a few times. Pour the mixture into the ice cream maker.
6. Connect the machine and press ice cream and the start button.
7. When the cycle is finished, transfer the sherbet to an airtight freezer-safe container or serve right away. The sherbet will be soft and creamy. If you like a harder texture, allow the sherbet to freeze for 2 hours or more before serving.

Without an ice cream maker

1. Place the granulated sugar, orange juice, and zest and vanilla extract in a high-speed blender or food processor.
2. Blitz until everything is combined and well incorporated and the sugar is fully dissolved.
3. Transfer the mixture into a clean bowl, preferably with a spout, and stir in the heavy cream and whole milk. Mix until everything is combined.

4. Pour the mixture into a Pyrex or stainless steel 9x13-inch pan. And place in the freezer for 30 minutes. The edges should start freezing. Using an electric handheld mixer, beat the Sherbet for 1 minute.
5. Return to the freezer for another 30 minutes and beat again as before. Do this same step 4-5 times until the Sherbet is harder.
6. Serve right away or transfer the Sherbet to an airtight freezer-safe container and serve it later.

Nutrition per Serving

Calories 478, fat 21 g, carbs 68 g, sugar 61 g
Protein 1 g, sodium 89 mg

Peach Sherbet

Makes about 4 cups (½ cup per serving)

Ingredients

1 cup light brown sugar
6 peaches, diced into bigger chunks
1 teaspoon vanilla extract
½ cup chilled heavy cream
½ cup chilled whole milk

Directions

With an ice cream maker

1. Freeze the ice cream maker bowl according to manufacturer instructions, usually 12 to 24 hours.
2. Meanwhile place the light brown sugar, peaches, and vanilla extract in a high-speed blender or food processor.
3. Blitz until everything is combined and well incorporated and the sugar is fully dissolved. It will take about 1 minute.
4. Transfer the mixture into a clean bowl, preferably with a spout, and stir in the heavy cream and whole milk. Mix until everything is combined.
5. Cover with plastic wrap and let it chill in the fridge for a minimum of 2 to 12 hours.
6. Pull out the sherbet mixture from the refrigerator and stir a few times.
7. Install the frozen ice cream maker bowl and pour the mixture into it.
8. Connect the machine and press ice cream and the start button.
9. When the cycle is finished, transfer the sherbet to an airtight freezer-safe container or serve right away. The sherbet will be soft and creamy. If you like a harder texture, allow the sherbet to freeze for 2 hours or more before serving.

Without an ice cream maker

1. Place the light brown sugar, peaches, and vanilla extract in a high-speed blender or food processor.
2. Blitz until everything is combined and well incorporated and the sugar is fully dissolved. It will take about 1 minute.
3. Transfer the mixture into a clean bowl, preferably with a spout, and stir in the heavy cream and whole milk. Mix until everything is combined.
4. Pour the mixture in a Pyrex or stainless steel 9x13-inch pan. And place in the freezer for 30 minutes. The edges should start freezing. Using an electric handheld mixer, beat the Sherbet for 1 minute.
5. Return to the freezer for another 30 minutes and beat again as before. Do this same step 4-5 times until the Sherbet is harder.
6. Serve right away or transfer the Sherbet to an airtight freezer-safe container and serve it later.

Nutrition per Serving
Calories 359, fat 12 g, carbs 61 g, sugar 57 g
Protein 3 g, sodium 98 mg

Blueberry Sherbet

Makes about 4 cups (½ cup per serving)

Ingredients

1 ½ cup granulated sugar
1 teaspoon vanilla extract
zest of 1 lemon
3 cups fresh or frozen blueberries
1 cup whole milk

Directions

With an ice cream maker

1. Freeze the ice cream maker bowl according to manufacturer instructions, usually 12 to 24 hours.
2. Meanwhile, place the sugar, lemon zest, blueberries, and vanilla extract in a high-speed blender or food processor.
3. Blitz until everything is combined and well incorporated and the sugar is fully dissolved. It will take about 1 minute.
4. Transfer the mixture into a clean bowl, preferably with a spout, and stir in the whole milk. Mix until everything is combined.
5. Cover with plastic wrap and let it chill in the fridge for about 2 to 12 hours.
6. Pull out the sherbet mixture from the refrigerator and stir a few times.
7. Install the frozen ice cream maker bowl and pour the mixture into it.
8. Connect the machine and press ice cream and the start button.
9. When the cycle is finished, transfer the sherbet to an airtight freezer-safe container or serve right away. The sherbet will be soft and creamy. If you like a harder texture, allow the sherbet to freeze for 2 hours or more before serving.

Without an ice cream maker

1. Place the sugar, lemon zest, blueberries, and vanilla extract in a high-speed blender or food processor.
2. Blitz until everything is combined and well incorporated and the sugar is fully dissolved. It will take about 1 minute.
3. Transfer the mixture into a clean bowl, preferably with a spout, and stir in the whole milk. Mix until everything is combined.
4. Pour the mixture in a Pyrex or stainless steel 9x13-inch pan and place it in the freezer for 30 minutes. The edges should start freezing. Using an electric handheld mixer, beat the Sherbet for 1 minute.
5. Return to the freezer for another 30 minutes and beat again as before. Do this same step 4-5 times until the Sherbet is harder.
6. Serve right away or transfer the Sherbet to an airtight freezer-safe container and serve it later.

Nutrition per Serving
Calories 387, fat 2 g, carbs 95 g, sugar 90 g
Protein 3 g, sodium 26 mg

Blood Orange Sherbet

Makes about 4 cups (½ cup per serving)

Ingredients

1 cup light corn syrup
zest of 1 bloody orange
2 cups freshly squeezed blood orange juice
1 teaspoon vanilla extract
1 cup whole milk

Directions

With an ice cream maker

1. Freeze the ice cream maker bowl according to manufacturer instructions, usually 12 to 24 hours.
2. Meanwhile, place the light corn syrup, blood orange juice, bloody orange zest, and vanilla extract in a high-speed blender or food processor.
3. Blitz until everything is combined and well incorporated.
4. Transfer the mixture into a clean bowl, preferably with a spout, and stir in the whole milk. Mix until everything is combined.
5. Cover with plastic wrap and let it chill in the fridge for about 2 to 12 hours.
6. Pull out the sherbet mixture from the refrigerator and stir a few times.
7. Install the frozen ice cream maker bowl and pour the mixture into it.
8. Connect the machine and press ice cream and the start button.
9. When the cycle is finished, transfer the sherbet to an airtight freezer-safe container or serve right away. The sherbet will be soft and creamy. If you like a harder texture, allow the sherbet to freeze for 2 hours or more before serving.

Without an ice cream maker

1. Place the light corn syrup, blood orange juice, bloody orange zest, and vanilla extract in a high-speed blender or food processor.
2. Blitz until everything is combined and well incorporated.
3. Transfer the mixture into a clean bowl, preferably with a spout, and stir in the whole milk. Mix until everything is combined.
4. Pour the mixture in a Pyrex or stainless steel 9x13-inch pan and place it in the freezer for 30 minutes. The edges should start freezing. Using an electric handheld mixer, beat the Sherbet for 1 minute.
5. Return to the freezer for another 30 minutes and beat again as before. Do this same step 4-5 times until the Sherbet is harder.
6. Serve right away or transfer the Sherbet to an airtight freezer-safe container and serve it later.

Nutrition per Serving
Calories 315, fat 2 g, carbs 75 g, sugar 34 g
Protein 3 g, sodium 27 mg

Lime Sherbet

Makes about 4 cups (½ cup per serving)

Ingredients
1 cup granulated sugar
zest of 2 limes
pinch of salt
¾ cup freshly squeezed lime juice
1 ½ cups whole milk
Green food coloring (optional)

Directions
With an ice cream maker

1. Freeze the ice cream maker bowl according to manufacturer instructions, usually 12 to 24 hours.
2. Meanwhile, place the granulated sugar, lime zest, salt, and lime juice in a high-speed blender or food processor.
3. Blitz until everything is combined and well incorporated and the sugar is fully dissolved. It will take about 1 minute.
4. Transfer the mixture into a clean bowl, preferably with a spout, and stir in the whole milk. Mix until everything is combined.
5. Cover with plastic wrap and let it chill in the fridge for about 2 to 12 hours.
6. Pull out the sherbet mixture from the refrigerator, add a few drops of green food coloring, if desired, and whisk to mix it well.
7. Install the frozen ice cream maker bowl and pour the mixture into it.
8. Connect the machine and press ice cream and the start button.
9. When the cycle is finished, transfer the sherbet to an airtight freezer-safe container or serve right away. The sherbet will be soft and creamy. If you like a harder texture, allow the sherbet to freeze for 2 hours or more before serving.

Without an ice cream maker

1. Place the granulated sugar, lime zest, salt, and lime juice in a high-speed blender or food processor.
2. Blitz until everything is combined and well incorporated and the sugar is fully dissolved. It will take about 1 minute.
3. Transfer the mixture into a clean bowl and stir in the whole milk and a few drops of the green food coloring, if desired.
4. Mix until everything is combined.
5. Pour the mixture in a Pyrex or stainless steel 9x13-inch pan and place it in the freezer for 30 minutes. The edges should start freezing. Using an electric handheld mixer, beat the Sherbet for 1 minute.

6. Return to the freezer for another 30 minutes and beat again as before. Do this same step 4-5 times until the Sherbet is harder.
7. Serve right away or transfer the Sherbet to an airtight freezer-safe container and serve it later.

Nutrition per Serving
Calories 249, fat 3 g, carbs 56.2 g, sugar 55.3 g
Protein 3.1 g, sodium 76 mg

Apricot Sherbet

Makes about 4 cups (½ cup per serving)

Ingredients

1 cup granulated sugar
1-pound apricots, seeded
1 teaspoon vanilla extract
1 cup whole milk

Directions

With an ice cream maker

1. Freeze the ice cream maker bowl according to manufacturer instructions, usually 12 to 24 hours.
2. Meanwhile, place the sugar, apricots, and vanilla extract in a high-speed blender or food processor.
3. Blitz until everything is combined and well incorporated.
4. Transfer the mixture into a clean bowl, preferably with a spout, and stir in the whole milk. Mix until everything is combined.
5. Cover with plastic wrap and let it chill in the fridge for about 2 to 12 hours.
6. Pull out the sherbet mixture from the refrigerator and whisk to mix it well.
7. Install the frozen ice cream maker bowl and pour the mixture into it.
8. Connect the machine and press ice cream and the start button.
9. When the cycle is finished, transfer the sherbet to an airtight freezer-safe container or serve right away. The sherbet will be soft and creamy. If you like a harder texture, allow the sherbet to freeze for 2 hours or more before serving.

Without an ice cream maker

1. Place the sugar, apricots, and vanilla extract in a high-speed blender or food processor. Blitz until everything is combined and well incorporated.
2. Transfer the mixture into a clean bowl and stir in the whole milk. Mix until everything is combined.
3. Pour the mixture in a Pyrex or stainless steel 9x13-inch pan and place it in the freezer for 30 minutes. The edges should start freezing. Using an electric handheld mixer, beat the Sherbet for 1 minute.
4. Return to the freezer for another 30 minutes and beat again as before. Do this same step 4-5 times until the Sherbet is harder.
5. Serve right away or transfer the Sherbet to an airtight freezer-safe container and serve it later.

Nutrition per Serving

Calories 281, fat 3 g, carbs 65 g, sugar 64 g
Protein 3 g, sodium 26 mg

Raspberry Sherbet

Makes about 4 cups (½ cup per serving)

Ingredients

1 cup granulated sugar
3 cups fresh raspberries
zest of 1 lemon
1 teaspoon vanilla extract
1 cup heavy cream

Directions

With an ice cream maker

1. Freeze the ice cream maker bowl according to manufacturer instructions, usually 12 to 24 hours.
2. Meanwhile, place the sugar, raspberries, lemon zest, and vanilla extract in a high-speed blender or food processor.
3. Blitz until everything is combined and well incorporated.
4. Transfer the mixture into a clean bowl, preferably with a spout, and stir in the heavy cream. Mix until combined.
5. Cover with plastic wrap and let it chill in the fridge for about 2 to 12 hours.
6. Pull out the sherbet mixture from the refrigerator and stir a few times.
7. Install the frozen ice cream maker bowl and pour the mixture into it.
8. Connect the machine and press ice cream and the start button.
9. When the cycle is finished, transfer the sherbet to an airtight freezer-safe container or serve right away. The sherbet will be soft and creamy. If you like a harder texture, allow the sherbet to freeze for 2 hours or more before serving.

Without an ice cream maker

1. Place the sugar, raspberries, lemon zest, and vanilla extract in a high-speed blender or food processor.
2. Blitz until everything is combined and well incorporated.
3. Transfer the mixture into a clean bowl and stir in the heavy cream. Mix until combined.
4. Pour the mixture in a Pyrex or stainless steel 9x13-inch pan. And place in the freezer for 30 minutes. The edges should start freezing. Using an electric handheld mixer, beat the Sherbet for 1 minute.
5. Return to the freezer for another 30 minutes and beat again as before. Do this same step 4-5 times until the Sherbet's texture is according to your taste.
6. Serve right away or transfer the Sherbet to an airtight freezer-safe container and serve it later.

Nutrition per Serving
Calories 342, fat 12 g, carbs 62 g, sugar 54 g
Protein 2 g, sodium 12 mg

Chocolate Sherbet

Makes about 4 cups (½ cup per serving)

Ingredients
1 cup light brown sugar
¾ cup cocoa powder
1 cup milk
½ teaspoon instant espresso powder
1 teaspoon vanilla extract
1 cup heavy cream

Directions
With an ice cream maker

1. Freeze the ice cream maker bowl according to manufacturer instructions, usually 12 to 24 hours.
2. Meanwhile, place the brown sugar, cocoa powder, milk, espresso powder, and vanilla extract in a high-speed blender or food processor.
3. Blitz until everything is combined and well incorporated.
4. Transfer the mixture into a clean bowl and stir in the heavy cream. Mix until combined.
5. Cover with plastic wrap and let it chill in the fridge for about 2 to 12 hours.
6. Pull out the sherbet mixture from the refrigerator and stir a few times.
7. Install the frozen ice cream maker bowl and pour the mixture into it.
8. Connect the machine and press ice cream and the start button.
9. When the cycle is finished, transfer the sherbet to an airtight freezer-safe container or serve right away. The sherbet will be soft and creamy. If you like a harder texture, allow the sherbet to freeze for 2 hours or more before serving.

Without an ice cream maker

1. Place the brown sugar, cocoa powder, milk, espresso powder, and vanilla extract in a high-speed blender or food processor.
2. Blitz until everything is combined and well incorporated.
3. Transfer the mixture into a clean bowl and stir in the heavy cream. Mix until combined.

4. Pour the mixture in a Pyrex or stainless steel 9x13-inch pan and place it in the freezer for 30 minutes. The edges should start freezing. Using an electric handheld mixer, beat the Sherbet for 1 minute.
5. Return to the freezer for another 30 minutes and beat again as before. Do this same step 4-5 times until the Sherbet's texture is according to your taste.
6. Serve right away or transfer the Sherbet to an airtight freezer-safe container and serve it later.

Nutrition per Serving

Calories 311, fat 15 g, carbs 48 g, sugar 38 g
Protein 6 g, sodium 53 mg

Pineapple Sherbet

Makes about 4 cups (½ cup per serving)

Ingredients

½ cup agave syrup
4 cups pineapple chunks
¾ cup milk
1 teaspoon vanilla extract
1 cup heavy cream

Directions

With an ice cream maker

1. Freeze the ice cream maker bowl according to manufacturer instructions, usually 12 to 24 hours.
2. Meanwhile, place the agave syrup, pineapple chunks, milk, and vanilla extract in a high-speed blender or food processor.
3. Blitz until everything is combined and well incorporated.
4. Transfer the mixture into a clean bowl, preferably with a spot, and stir in the heavy cream.
5. Mix until combined.
6. Cover with plastic wrap and let it chill in the fridge for about 2 to 12.
7. Pull out the sherbet mixture from the refrigerator and stir a few times.
8. Install the frozen ice cream maker bowl and pour the mixture into it.
9. Connect the machine and press ice cream and the start button.
10. When the cycle is finished, transfer the sherbet to an airtight freezer-safe container or serve right away. The sherbet will be soft and creamy. If you like a harder texture, allow the sherbet to freeze for 2 hours or more before serving.

Without an ice cream maker

1. Place the agave syrup, pineapple chunks, milk, and vanilla extract in a high-speed blender or food processor.
2. Blitz until everything is combined and well incorporated.
3. Transfer the mixture into a clean bowl and stir in the heavy cream.
4. Mix until combined.
5. Pour the mixture in a Pyrex or stainless steel 9x13-inch pan. And place in the freezer for 30 minutes. The edges should start freezing. Using an electric handheld mixer, beat the Sherbet for 1 minute.
6. Return to the freezer for another 30 minutes and beat again as before. Do this same step 4-5 times until the Sherbet's texture is according to your taste.
7. Serve right away or transfer the Sherbet to an airtight freezer-safe container and serve it later.

Nutrition per Serving
Calories 337, fat 12 g, carbs 58 g, sugar 19 g
Protein 3 g, sodium 63 mg

Pineapple and Coconut Sherbet

Makes about 4 cups (½ cup per serving)

Ingredients

1 cup granulated sugar
4 cups pineapple chunks
¾ cup coconut milk
1 teaspoon vanilla extract
1 cup heavy cream
½ cup coconut flakes

Directions

With an ice cream maker

1. Freeze the ice cream maker bowl according to manufacturer instructions, usually 12 to 24 hours.
2. Meanwhile, place the sugar, pineapple chunks, coconut milk, and vanilla extract in a high-speed blender or food processor.
3. Blitz until everything is combined and well incorporated.
4. Transfer the mixture into a clean bowl, preferably with a spout, and stir in the heavy cream. Mix until combined.
5. Cover with plastic wrap and let it chill in the fridge for about 2 to 12 hours.
6. Pull out the sherbet mixture from the refrigerator and stir a few times.
7. Install the frozen ice cream maker bowl and pour the mixture into it.
8. Connect the machine and press ice cream and the start button.
9. About 5 to 6 minutes before then end of the churning process, add the coconut flakes little by little into the sherbet and let them mix in.
10. When the cycle is finished, transfer the sherbet to an airtight freezer-safe container or serve right away. The sherbet will be soft and creamy. If you like a harder texture, allow the sherbet to freeze for 2 hours or more before serving.

Without an ice cream maker

1. Place the sugar, pineapple chunks, coconut milk, and vanilla extract in a high-speed blender or food processor.
2. Blitz until everything is combined and well incorporated.
3. Transfer the mixture into a clean bowl and stir in the heavy cream.
4. Mix until combined.
5. Pour the mixture in a Pyrex or stainless steel 9x13-inch pan. And place in the freezer for 30 minutes. The edges should start freezing. Using an electric handheld mixer, beat the sherbet for 1 minute.
6. Return to the freezer for another 30 minutes and beat again as before. Do this same step 4-5 times until the Sherbet's texture is according to your taste.

7. Serve right away or transfer the sherbet to an airtight freezer-safe container and serve it later.

Nutrition per Serving
Calories 480, fat 22 g, carbs 75 g, sugar 68 g
Protein 3 g, sodium 3 mg

FROZEN YOGURT RECIPES

Blueberry Frozen Yogurt

Makes about 4 cups (½ cup per serving)

Ingredients

2 ripe bananas

1 cup frozen blueberries

½ teaspoon vanilla extract

1 cup full-fat Greek Yogurt

Directions

With an ice cream maker

1. Freeze the ice cream maker bowl according to manufacturer instructions, usually 12 to 24 hours.
2. Place the bananas, blueberries, Greek yogurt, and vanilla extract in a high-speed blender or food processor until creamy and thick mixture forms.
3. Cover with plastic wrap and let it chill in the fridge for about 2 to 12 hours.
4. Pull out the yogurt mixture from the refrigerator and stir a few times.
5. Install the frozen ice cream maker bowl and pour the mixture into it.
6. Connect the machine and press Frozen Yogurt and the start button.
7. When the cycle is finished, transfer the yogurt to an airtight freezer-safe container or serve right away.

Without an ice cream maker

1. Place the banana and blueberry fruit, Greek yogurt, and vanilla extract in a high-speed blender or food processor until creamy and thick mixture forms.
2. Pour the mixture in a Pyrex or stainless steel 9x13-inch pan. And place in the freezer for 30 minutes. The edges should start freezing. Using an electric handheld mixer, beat the Greek Yogurt for 1 minute.
3. Return to the freezer for another 30 minutes and beat again as before. Do this same step 4-5 times until the Frozen yogurt is harder.
4. Serve right away or transfer the Frozen yogurt to an airtight freezer-safe container and serve it later.

Nutrition per Serving

Calories 79, fat 3 g, carbs 13 g, sugar 7 g

Protein 1 g, sodium 1 mg

Mango Frozen Yogurt

Makes about 4 cups (½ cup per serving)

Ingredients

1 pound peeled and diced mango
1 ½ cup Greek yogurt
½ cup heavy cream
1 teaspoon vanilla extract
3 tablespoons honey

Directions

With an ice cream maker

1. Freeze the ice cream maker bowl according to manufacturer instructions, usually 12 to 24 hours.
2. Place the diced mango, honey, and Greek yogurt in a blender or food processor.
3. Pour the mango puree in a clean bowl, preferably with a spout, and stir in the heavy cream and vanilla extract.
4. Cover with plastic wrap and let it chill in the fridge for about 2 to 12 hours.
5. Pull out the yogurt mixture from the refrigerator and stir a few times.
6. Install the frozen ice cream maker bowl and pour the mixture into it.
7. Connect the machine and press Frozen Yogurt and the start button.
8. When the cycle is finished, transfer the yogurt to an airtight freezer-safe container or serve right away.

Without an ice cream maker

1. Place the diced mango, honey, and Greek yogurt in a blender or food processor.
2. Stir in the heavy cream and vanilla extract.
3. Pour the Frozen Yogurt mixture in a Pyrex or stainless steel 9x13-inch pan and place it in the freezer for 30 minutes. The edges should start freezing. Using an electric handheld mixer, beat the Greek Yogurt for 1 minute.
4. Return to the freezer for another 30 minutes and beat again as before. Do this same step 4-5 times until the Frozen yogurt is harder.
5. Serve right away or transfer the Frozen yogurt to an airtight freezer-safe container and serve it later.

Nutrition per Serving

Calories 219, fat 10 g, carbs 32 g, sugar 27 g
Protein 4 g, sodium 8 mg

Lemon Frozen Yogurt

Makes about 4 cups (½ cup per serving)

Ingredients
4 cups Greek Yogurt
1 cup granulated sugar
½ cup freshly squeezed lemon juice
1 tablespoon freshly grated lemon zest

Directions
With an ice cream maker

1. Freeze the ice cream maker bowl according to manufacturer instructions, usually 12 to 24 hours.
2. Meanwhile in a large mixing bowl, add the Greek yogurt, granulated sugar, and stir until all the sugar is dissolved.
3. Stir in the lemon juice and lemon zest. Mix until combined.
4. Cover the bowl with plastic wrap and let it chill in the fridge for about 2 to 12 hours.
5. Pull out the yogurt mixture from the refrigerator and stir a few times.
6. Install the frozen ice cream maker bowl and pour the mixture into it.
7. Connect the machine and press Frozen Yogurt and the start button.
8. When the cycle is finished, transfer the yogurt to an airtight freezer-safe container or serve right away.

Without an ice cream maker

1. In a large mixing bowl, add the Greek yogurt, granulated sugar, and stir until all the sugar is dissolved.
2. Stir in the lemon juice and lemon zest. Mix until combined.
3. Pour the Frozen Yogurt mixture in a Pyrex or stainless steel 9x13-inch pan and place it in the freezer for 30 minutes. The edges should start freezing. Using an electric handheld mixer, beat the Greek Yogurt for 1 minute.
4. Return to the freezer for another 30 minutes and beat again as before. Do this same step 4-5 times until the Frozen yogurt hardens.
5. Serve right away or transfer the Frozen yogurt to an airtight freezer-safe container and serve it later.

Nutrition per Serving
Calories 326, fat 10 g, carbs 54 g, sugar 51 g
Protein 7 g, sodium 6 mg

Kiwi Frozen Yogurt

Makes about 4 cups (½ cup per serving)

Ingredients

3 cups Greek Yogurt
1 pound kiwi, peeled and diced in bigger chunks
1 cup granulated sugar
½ teaspoon vanilla extract
2 tablespoons lemon juice

Directions

With an ice cream maker

1. Freeze the ice cream maker bowl according to manufacturer instructions, usually 12 to 24 hours.
2. Place the diced kiwis, granulated sugar, and Greek yogurt in a blender or food processor.
3. Blitz until fully combined and puree forms and transfer the mixture to a clean bowl.
4. Stir in the vanilla extract and lemon juice.
5. Cover with plastic wrap and let it chill in the fridge for about 2 to 12 hours.
6. Pull out the yogurt mixture from the refrigerator and stir a few times.
7. Install the frozen ice cream maker bowl and pour the mixture into it.
8. Connect the machine and press Frozen Yogurt and the start button.
9. When the cycle is finished, transfer the yogurt to an airtight freezer-safe container or serve right away.

Without an ice cream maker

1. Place the diced kiwis, granulated sugar, and Greek yogurt in a blender or food processor.
2. Blitz until fully combined and puree forms and transfer the mixture to a clean bowl.
3. Stir in the vanilla extract and lemon juice.
4. Pour the Frozen Yogurt mixture in a Pyrex or stainless steel 9x13-inch pan. And place in the freezer for 30 minutes. The edges should start freezing. Using an electric handheld mixer, beat the Greek Yogurt for 1 minute.
5. Return to the freezer for another 30 minutes and beat again as before. Do this same step 4-5 times until the Frozen yogurt hardens.
6. Serve right away or transfer the Frozen yogurt to an airtight freezer-safe container and serve it later.

Nutrition per Serving

Calories 358, fat 8 g, carbs 69 g, sugar 60 g
Protein 7 g, sodium 5 mg

Orange Frozen Yogurt

Makes about 4 cups (½ cup per serving)

Ingredients
4 cups Greek Yogurt
1 teaspoon vanilla extract
1 cup granulated sugar
zest of 1 orange
1 cup freshly squeezed orange juice

Directions
With an ice cream maker

1. Freeze the ice cream maker bowl according to manufacturer instructions, usually 12 to 24 hours.
2. Place the Greek yogurt and vanilla extract in a high-speed blender or food processor and add in the sugar, orange juice, and orange zest.
3. Blitz until creamy and well-combined mixture forms.
4. Pour the mixture in a clean bowl, preferably with a spout.
5. Cover with plastic wrap and let it chill in the fridge for about 2 to 12 hours.
6. Pull out the yogurt mixture from the refrigerator and stir a few times.
7. Install the frozen ice cream maker bowl and pour the mixture into it.
8. Connect the machine and press Frozen Yogurt and the start button.
9. When the cycle is finished, transfer the yogurt to an airtight freezer-safe container or serve right away.

Without an ice cream maker

1. Place the Greek yogurt and vanilla extract in a high-speed blender or food processor and add in the sugar, orange juice, and orange zest.
2. Blitz until creamy and well-combined mixture forms.
3. Pour the mixture in a Pyrex or stainless steel 9x13-inch pan and place it in the freezer for 30 minutes. The edges should start freezing. Using an electric handheld mixer, beat the Greek Yogurt for 1 minute.
4. Return to the freezer for another 30 minutes and beat again as before. Do this same step 4-5 times until the Frozen yogurt is harder.
5. Serve right away or transfer the Frozen yogurt to an airtight freezer-safe container and serve it later.

Nutrition per Serving
Calories 350, fat 10 g, carbs 60 g, sugar 55 g
Protein 7 g, sodium 1 mg

Strawberry Frozen Yogurt

Makes about 4 cups (½ cup per serving)

Ingredients
4 cups Greek Yogurt
1 teaspoon vanilla extract
1 cup light brown sugar
zest of 1 lime
3 tablespoons lime juice
2 cups strawberries, diced

Directions
With an ice cream maker

1. Freeze the ice cream maker bowl according to manufacturer instructions, usually 12 to 24 hours.
2. Place the Greek yogurt and vanilla extract in a high-speed blender or food processor and add in the light brown sugar, lime zest, and lime juice.
3. Blitz until creamy and well-combined mixture forms.
4. Add in the strawberries and blitz again until creamy and well-combined. Pour the whole mixture in a clean bowl, preferably with a spout.
5. Cover with plastic wrap and let it chill in the fridge for about 2 to 12 hours.
6. Pull out the yogurt mixture from the refrigerator and stir a few times.
7. Install the frozen ice cream maker bowl and pour the mixture into it.
8. Connect the machine and press Frozen Yogurt and the start button.
9. When the cycle is finished, transfer the yogurt to an airtight freezer-safe container or serve right away.

Without an ice cream maker

1. Place the Greek yogurt and vanilla extract in a high-speed blender or food processor and add in the light brown sugar, lime zest, and lime juice.
2. Blitz until creamy and well-combined mixture forms.
3. Add in the strawberries and blitz again until creamy and well-combined.
4. Pour the mixture in a Pyrex or stainless steel 9x13-inch pan and place it in the freezer for 30 minutes. The edges should start freezing. Using an electric handheld mixer, beat the Greek Yogurt for 1 minute.
5. Return to the freezer for another 30 minutes and beat again as before. Do this same step 4-5 times until the Frozen yogurt hardens.
6. Serve right away or transfer the Frozen yogurt to an airtight freezer-safe container and serve it later.

Nutrition per Serving
Calories 303, fat 10 g, carbs 47 g, sugar 39 g
Protein 8 g, sodium 12 mg

Raspberry Frozen Yogurt

Makes about 4 cups (½ cup per serving)

Ingredients
4 cups Greek Yogurt
1 teaspoon vanilla extract
½ cup honey
pinch of salt
2 cups fresh or frozen raspberries
zest of 1 lemon
Directions
With an ice cream maker

1. Freeze the ice cream maker bowl according to manufacturer instructions, usually 12 to 24 hours.
2. Place the Greek yogurt and vanilla extract in a high-speed blender or food processor and add in the honey, salt, raspberries, and lemon zest.
3. Blitz until creamy and well-combined mixture forms.
4. Pour the whole mixture in a clean bowl, preferably with a spout.
5. Cover with plastic wrap and let it chill in the fridge for about 2 to 12 hours.
6. Pull out the yogurt mixture from the refrigerator and stir a few times.
7. Install the frozen ice cream maker bowl and pour the mixture into it.
8. Connect the machine and press Frozen Yogurt and the start button.
9. When the cycle is finished, transfer the yogurt to an airtight freezer-safe container or serve right away.

Without an ice cream maker

1. Place the Greek yogurt and vanilla extract in a high-speed blender or food processor and add in the honey, salt, raspberries, and lemon zest.
2. Blitz until creamy and well-combined mixture forms.
3. Pour the mixture in a Pyrex or stainless steel 9x13-inch pan and place it in the freezer for 30 minutes. The edges should start freezing. Using an electric handheld mixer, beat the Greek Yogurt for 1 minute.
4. Return to the freezer for another 30 minutes and beat again as before. Do this same step 4-5 times until the Frozen yogurt hardens.

5. Serve right away or transfer the Frozen yogurt to an airtight freezer-safe container and serve it later.

Nutrition per Serving

Calories 395, fat 10 g, carbs 72 g, sugar 63 g
Protein 8 g, sodium 42 mg

Coconut Frozen Yogurt

Makes about 4 cups (½ cup per serving)

Ingredients
4 cups coconut-flavored Greek Yogurt
1 teaspoon vanilla extract
1 cup powdered sugar
3 tablespoons canned coconut milk
¼ cup coconut flakes

Directions
With an ice cream maker

1. Freeze the ice cream maker bowl according to manufacturer instructions, usually 12 to 24 hours.
2. Place the coconut flavored Greek yogurt, vanilla extract, powdered sugar, and coconut milk in a high-speed blender or food processor.
3. Blitz until creamy and well-combined mixture forms.
4. Pour the mixture in a clean bowl, preferably with a spout.
5. Cover with plastic wrap and let it chill in the fridge for about 2 to 12 hours.
6. Pull out the yogurt mixture from the refrigerator and stir a few times.
7. Install the frozen ice cream maker bowl and pour the mixture into it.
8. Connect the machine and press Frozen Yogurt and the start button.
9. About 5 or 6 minutes before the end of the churning cycle, add the coconut flakes little by little and let it mix in.
10. When the cycle is finished, transfer the yogurt to an airtight freezer-safe container or serve right away.

Without an ice cream maker

1. Place the coconut flavored Greek yogurt, vanilla extract, powdered sugar, coconut flakes, and coconut milk in a high-speed blender or food processor.
2. Blitz until creamy and well-combined mixture forms.
3. Pour the mixture in a Pyrex or stainless steel 9x13-inch pan and place it in the freezer for 30 minutes. The edges should start freezing. Using an electric handheld mixer, beat the Greek Yogurt for 1 minute.
4. Return to the freezer for another 30 minutes and beat again as before. Do this same step 4-5 times until the Frozen yogurt hardens.
5. Serve right away or transfer the Frozen yogurt to an airtight freezer-safe container and serve it later.

Nutrition per Serving

Calories 276, fat 13 g, carbs 34 g, sugar 30 g
Protein 7 g, sodium 2 mg

Chocolate Protein Frozen Yogurt

Makes about 4 cups (½ cup per serving)

Ingredients

3 cups Greek Yogurt
1 teaspoon vanilla extract
1 teaspoon instant espresso powder
1 cup granulated sugar
½ cup cocoa powder
2 tablespoons chocolate protein powder

Directions

With an ice cream maker

1. Freeze the ice cream maker bowl according to manufacturer instructions, usually 12 to 24 hours.
2. Place the Greek yogurt, vanilla extract, instant espresso powder, granulated sugar, cocoa powder, and chocolate protein powder in a high-speed blender or food processor.
3. Blitz until creamy and well-combined mixture forms.
4. Pour the mixture into a clean bowl, preferably with a spout.
5. Cover with plastic wrap and let it chill in the fridge for about 2 to 12 hours.
6. Pull out the yogurt mixture from the refrigerator and stir a few times.
7. Install the frozen ice cream maker bowl and pour the mixture into it.
8. Connect the machine and press Frozen Yogurt and the start button.
9. When the cycle is finished, transfer the yogurt to an airtight freezer-safe container or serve right away.

Without an ice cream maker

1. Place the Greek yogurt, vanilla extract, instant espresso powder, granulated sugar, cocoa powder, and chocolate protein powder in a high-speed blender or food processor.
2. Blitz until creamy and well-combined mixture forms.
3. Pour the mixture in a Pyrex or stainless steel 9x13-inch pan and place it in the freezer for 30 minutes. The edges should start freezing. Using an electric handheld mixer, beat the Greek Yogurt for 1 minute.
4. Return to the freezer for another 30 minutes and beat again as before. Do this same step 4-5 times until the Frozen yogurt hardens.
5. Serve right away or transfer the Frozen yogurt to an airtight freezer-safe container and serve it later.

Nutrition per Serving
Calories 367, fat 10 g, carbs 60 g, sugar 51 g
Protein 17 g, sodium 82 mg

Vanilla Frozen Yogurt

Makes about 4 cups (½ cup per serving)

Ingredients

3 cups Greek Yogurt
2 teaspoons vanilla extract
1 cup granulated sugar
pinch of salt

Directions

With an ice cream maker

1. Freeze the ice cream maker bowl according to manufacturer instructions, usually 12 to 24 hours.
2. Place the Greek yogurt, vanilla extract, granulated sugar, and pinch of salt in a high-speed blender or food processor.
3. Blitz until creamy and well-combined mixture forms.
4. Pour the mixture in a clean bowl, preferably with a spout.
5. Cover with plastic wrap and let it chill in the fridge for about 2 to 12 hours.
6. Pull out the yogurt mixture from the refrigerator and stir a few times.
7. Install the frozen ice cream maker bowl and pour the mixture into it.
8. Connect the machine and press Frozen Yogurt and the start button.
9. When the cycle is finished, transfer the yogurt to an airtight freezer-safe container or serve right away.

Without an ice cream maker

1. Place the Greek yogurt, vanilla extract, granulated sugar, and pinch of salt in a high-speed blender or food processor.
2. Blitz until creamy and well-combined mixture forms.
3. Pour the mixture in a Pyrex or stainless steel 9x13-inch pan and place it in the freezer for 30 minutes. The edges should start freezing. Using an electric handheld mixer, beat the Greek Yogurt for 1 minute.
4. Return to the freezer for another 30 minutes and beat again as before. Do this same step 4-5 times until the Frozen yogurt hardens.
5. Serve right away or transfer the Frozen yogurt to an airtight freezer-safe container and serve it later.

Nutrition per Serving

Calories 291, fat 8 g, carbs 53 g, sugar 50 g
Protein 5 g, sodium 39 mg

RECIPE INDEX

APPENDIX

Cooking Conversion Charts

1. Measuring Equivalent Chart

Type	Imperial	Imperial	Metric
Weight	1 dry ounce		28g
	1 pound	16 dry ounces	0.45 kg
Volume	1 teaspoon		5 ml
	1 dessert spoon	2 teaspoons	10 ml
	1 tablespoon	3 teaspoons	15 ml
	1 Australian tablespoon	4 teaspoons	20 ml
	1 fluid ounce	2 tablespoons	30 ml
	1 cup	16 tablespoons	240 ml
	1 cup	8 fluid ounces	240 ml
	1 pint	2 cups	470 ml
	1 quart	2 pints	0.95 l
	1 gallon	4 quarts	3.8 l
Length	1 inch		2.54 cm

Numbers are rounded to the closest equivalent

Printed in Great Britain
by Amazon